Evangelicalism Is Dead

Evangelicalism Is Dead

PAUL O. BISCHOFF

RESOURCE *Publications* • Eugene, Oregon

EVANGELICALISM IS DEAD

Copyright © 2020 Paul O. Bischoff. All rights reserved. Except for brief quotations in critical publications or reviews, no part of this book may be reproduced in any manner without prior written permission from the publisher. Write: Permissions, Wipf and Stock Publishers, 199 W. 8th Ave., Suite 3, Eugene, OR 97401.

Resource Publications
An Imprint of Wipf and Stock Publishers
199 W. 8th Ave., Suite 3
Eugene, OR 97401

www.wipfandstock.com

PAPERBACK ISBN: 978-1-7252-5861-7
HARDCOVER ISBN: 978-1-7252-5862-4
EBOOK ISBN: 978-1-7252-5863-1

Manufactured in the U.S.A.   JANUARY 28, 2020

To the Adult Forum members of the
First Presbyterian Church in Wheaton, Illinois

Contents

Preface ix

Introduction 1

Chapter 1 The Gospel 7

Chapter 2 The Church 15

Chapter 3 Gnosticism and Christianity 26

Chapter 4 The Reformation and Protestantism 33

Chapter 5 The Puritans and the Pietists 39

Chapter 6 Cane Ridge and the Great Awakenings 46

Chapter 7 Classic Evangelicalism 54

Chapter 8 Evangelicalism and Gnosticism 67

Chapter 9 Fundamentalism 76

Chapter 10 New Evangelicalism 84

Chapter 11 Contemporary and Emergent Evangelicalism 92

Chapter 12 The Death of Evangelicalism 100

Chapter 13 The Twenty-First Century Church 107

Conclusion 115

Bibliography 119

Preface

EVANGELICALISM IS DEAD. It died peacefully surrounded by its family of associations, alliances, and coalitions. No churches were there. A white evangelist was sought to bring the eulogy, but none could be found. Evangelical leaders wanted a mega-church pastor to do the funeral, but the best-known ones were embroiled in embezzlement or sex scandals. The National Association of Evangelicals wanted the bulletin to read, "Celebrating the Life of Evangelicalism and a Witness to the Resurrection of Jesus Christ." However, this was voted down because it might offend seekers. The bulletin read, "Celebrating the Life of Evangelicalism and a Witness to Self-Satisfied Spirituality." Donations were made to the Coalition for Experiential Religion in America. The media reported that the funeral service seemed more like a political rally than a reverential worship service. There were no Christian symbols in the theater hosting the celebration. Projection and sound systems often failed during the service. Many who attended expressed being born again, but had no church affiliation. The Religious-Culture Alliance credited Evangelicalism for accommodating current models of business leadership, drama, and concert formats into its liturgy. Many thanked Evangelicalism for helping them to be spiritual without being religious. Leading postmodern Evangelical pastors credited God's love for helping them shed out-of-date teachings like sin, the cross, and hell. Nationally-known therapists affirmed the deceased for helping Americans feel good about themselves. One woman said she searched for

Preface

Evangelicalism, but no one could tell her where to find it. Could it be that Evangelicalism existed only in the minds of its adherents?

This book gets into how Evangelicalism ironically tried to revive a dead church, but failed because it left the church. Once out of the church, it was homeless. To sustain its existence it became a parasite on the church. Wanting to be relevant, it attached itself to culture. Evangelicalism constantly reinvented itself by engaging and accommodating its surrounding culture—a Gnostic culture. These two "isms" had much in common—individualism, self-righteousness and spiritual pride. Eventually, a twenty-first Gnostic culture absorbed such that one couldn't tell where the church began and culture ended.

Evangelicalism became sick. The diagnosis was "lost identity." Relevance was prescribed to no avail. Its final attempt at recovery included affiliation with conservative politics which failed due to moral failures of right-wing political leaders. Hospice professionals were called in to administer palliative care.

But Evangelicalism died. Many mourned. Few expressed hope for its resurrection. Some even thought its death was a blessing.

Evangel still means good news, the gospel. *Evangelical* may once again achieve its original status from the Reformation. The healing gospel may rejoin and minister to a damaged church. A church reformed by the Word of God and revived by the Holy Spirit may yet flourish in the twenty-first century. The death of Evangelicalism is a blessing.

The book is an outgrowth of the questions and thoughts from a series of presentations during an adult forum at the First Presbyterian Church in Wheaton, Illinois conducted in the fall of 2019. Other contributors include Rev. Shelly Satran, Senior Pastor of Faith Evangelical Lutheran Church in Glen Ellyn, Illinois whose sermons have significantly influenced my understanding of the gospel and the church. Julius Jackson, Minister of Lebanon Baptist Church in Chicago, and his congregation have affirmed my instincts about how the non-white church in general and the African-American church in particular offer hope for Christianity's future in America. Special thanks to confreres Tom Hill and Grant

Preface

Lantz for their always-substantive comments throughout the writing process. My wife Jayne continues to be my patient sounding board and faithful encourager.

November 24, 2019
Paul O. Bischoff
The Feast of Christ, the King
Wheaton

Introduction

THIS BOOK IS ABOUT EVANGELICALISM, a three-hundred-year-old religious movement whose followers see themselves as a special type of Christian. *Evangelicalism*, a noun, is a religious movement not to be confused with *evangel*. *Evangel*, a noun, is derived from the Greek word for gospel—the life, death and, resurrection of Jesus Christ. *Evangelical*, an adjective, describes a person or religious organization adhering to Evangelicalism's principles. The terms *Evangelicalism* and *Evangelical* defy clarity. Only *evangel* is clearly defined as the good news of the gospel. This book attempts to explain how and why Evangelicalism originated in the early church, left it, drifted away from biblical Christianity, accommodated a Gnostic culture, and eventually died.

Chapter 1 defines the gospel with Jesus' words: "The kingdom of God is near. Repent and believe the good news!"[1] The gospel is an interaction of the kingdom, repentance, and belief whose objective is to help people love God with all one's strength, mind, soul, and spirit. The book shows how Jesus assigned faith and salvation to those whom he encountered often without a so-called conversion experience. The gospel and the church collaborate together in the process of salvation. A community of people is not the church without the gospel. The gospel's proclamation originates and continues only through the church. A person's conversion is consummated by participation in the body of Christ, the church.

1. Mark 1:15

Chapter 2 defines the church as a community of recovering sinners. This chapter asserts that *there is no salvation outside the church*. Not a particular church, tradition, denomination, or movement. But by participation in the body of Christ, the church. Individual decisions to follow Jesus as Lord make no sense if not followed by joining a local congregation of believers, the church. The church is *the* tradition of the Christian faith. This chapter traces the evolution of church history referencing Scripture, reformers Luther and Calvin, with interpretation by Barth and Bonhoeffer.

Chapter 3 exposes Gnosticism as the church's oldest heresy. It is a dualism between matter and spirit, where matter is considered evil and only spirit is good. We object to the notion of a divine spark within every person which is enflamed through special knowledge for salvation. This chapter dismantles Gnosticism's anti-body ideology and proposes a theology of the body from the creation of human beings in the image of God and the Apostle Paul's theology of the church as the body of Christ.

Chapter 4 discusses Evangelicalism's origin in the Reformation and Luther's use of *Evangelical* to identify those persons who adhere to a Christ-centered life and Scripture-based faith. To be Evangelical in the sixteenth century meant to be an active member of the church. We note that Luther never left the church or minimized its essential meaning for all Christians. We explain why the Reformation was not Protestant, a political term never used by Luther. We state that the Reformation is the first and last usage of *Evangelical* in church history to mean the gospel as kingdom, repentance and belief within the church.

Chapter 5 discusses two European church movements which have informed Evangelicalism. Puritanism tried to purify the Church of England both doctrinally and spiritually. Puritans came to the New World to escape religious persecution. Pietism, a departure from German Lutheran doctrinal orthodoxy, left the church to form its own special little renewal groups. Most scholars today assert that Pietism's influence on Evangelicalism outweighed that of Puritanism. Both movements left the church, departed from the theological moorings of the Reformation, and shaped

INTRODUCTION

Evangelicalism as an individualistic experienced-based parachurch movement.

Chapter 6 analyzes how the Great Awakenings in America impacted Evangelicalism. Tree-surrounded spaces became the new sanctuaries where individuals had unique spiritual experiences some of which included authentic encounters with God. Of particular note is the Cane Ridge Awakening[2] which characterized the revivalism of Jonathan Edwards and George Whitefield. Such mass experiences often included swooning, inner feelings of warmth, dancing, barking, and collapsing. This chapter addresses how the authority given to inner mystical experience weakened Scripture's influence on Evangelicalism. Spiritual experience was now *the* criterion for being saved.

Chapter 7 is the climax of the book. It analyzes David Bebbington's familiar definition of Evangelicalism using the four terms: *conversionism, biblicism, crucicentrism,* and *activism*.[3] We pay special attention to conversion as the key criterion for being an Evangelical. Here we note Evangelicalism's excessive reliance on the born-again experience as the *sine qua non* of Christian faith. This chapter concludes with an analysis of several New Testament texts and input from respected authors who advance grace-based obedience based upon faith rooted in a Christ-crucified message as the basis for becoming Jesus-followers. We assert that Evangelicalism was the wolf of a distorted gospel masked by a sheep's spiritual clothing.

Chapter 8 discusses Evangelicalism's Gnostic vulnerabilities. The book proposes a holistic theology of salvation including a theology of the body to replace Evangelicalism's inability to embrace the body's redemption. It fails to view human beings as an integration of body, mind, soul, and spirit all of which are redeemed by Christ. It minimizes the church as the concrete body of Christ. Gnostic dualism is exposed as a negative contribution to Evangelicalism's theological distortions of a person, salvation, and the church. Jesus redeemed whole persons who were to love God,

---

2. Bloom, *American Religion*, 33.
3. Noll, *Rise of Evangelicalism*, 19.

neighbor, and self in the biblical sense of love. Christians are not abstract converts as bodiless souls. Genuine Jesus followers participate in the concrete body of Christ, the church.

Chapter 9 gets into Fundamentalism as an early twentieth-century form of Gnosticism. This sub-movement attempted to protect the supernatural aspects of the Christian faith stripped away by modernism and theological liberalism. It withdrew from culture. Fundamentalism reduced Christianity to five essentials: the inerrancy of the Bible, the reality of miracles, the virgin birth, Jesus' bodily resurrection, and the substitutionary atonement. It was a militant defense of the faith unnecessarily expressed in anger, while withdrawing into the piety of its own separatist subculture. Its desired protection of the supernatural was hampered by its anti-intellectualism.

Chapter 10 analyzes a reactive movement called New Evangelicalism. It was an attempt to atone for Fundamentalism's withdrawal from culture and mindlessness. Neo-Evangelicalism tried to meet humanists and liberal intellectuals on their own turf and gave birth to periodicals, seminaries and the mass revivals of Billy Graham. Evangelicalism "came of age." It was now professional. It sought to engage culture by worshiping at the altar of relevance creating space for later movements which unashamedly put the church in harm's way by accommodating Gnostic culture.

Chapter 11 discusses two Gnostic emanations of Evangelicalism: the Contemporary and Emergent Church movements. Just as Neo-Evangelicalism engaged culture, these two movements opposed one another while demonstrating their skill at accommodating culture into their churches. The Contemporary movement split the church into liturgy-based factions designed to provide customer satisfaction. The Sunday morning event traded mass evangelism for Christian worship. The revivals from the forests came inside. The Emergent Church, reacting against the Contemporary movement, resurrected ancient liturgies, minimized doctrine, and reveled in endless conversations without theological content. No church uses *Emergent* in its signage today. The Emergent conversation lived about twenty years.

INTRODUCTION

Chapter 12 summarizes the reasons for Evangelicalism's death. First, we summarize Gnosticism's core concepts. Second, we summarize the major tenets of the gospel and church. Third, we list ways in which a naïve Gnostic-influenced Evangelicalism unwittingly, and I believe unintentionally, distorted the gospel and the church. The sad fact is that its intentions were noble and, frankly, needed in order to reform and revive the church. But just as a catalyst is effective only as a short-lived boost in a chemical reaction, so also Evangelicalism should have only been temporary. Jesus of Nazareth's life on earth was temporary leaving behind a church which continues today. Homeless Evangelicalism never understood that its purpose was corrective, not normal. It was never supposed to take on a life of its own. It left only distortion and confusion in its wake. Evangelicalism imploded in its misguided attempt to engage and accommodate culture. It was absorbed by culture—a Gnostic culture. It failed to transform culture; a task never mandated by Scripture. Its re-invention only appeared successful in the political polls. The loss of its first love led to its death.

Chapter 13 ends the discussion on a note of hope for the twenty-first-century church. We analyze how the church needs to recover from Evangelicalism. The church must call out its demons of self-centeredness, narcissism and neglect of God's Word. The gospel must be reclaimed as kingdom, repentance, and belief in Jesus Christ as Lord. Christianity must reconceive the person as an integration of body, mind, soul, and spirit created in God's image, tainted by sin, and redeemed only by the necessary and sufficient sacrifice of Jesus on a cross. Since Jesus Christ is alive, the gospel and the church have a chance not only to survive but also to flourish. But this can occur only after the Benediction at Evangelicalism's graveside.

Chapter 1

The Gospel

JESUS SAID, "THE KINGDOM OF GOD IS NEAR. Repent and believe the good news." He defined the gospel as the collaboration of three elements—the kingdom, repentance, and belief. We assert that he gospel cannot be confined only to an individual and that the church as a community has no meaning without the gospel. There is no individual salvation outside the church. There is no church without the gospel message. These statements are the threads that hold the tapestry of this book together.

The gospel has Jewish roots. Kingdom, repentance, and belief are derived from the Law and the Prophets which Jesus came to fulfill. David's final prayer before handing the nation over to Solomon stated that the kingdom was the Lord's and that he was exalted as head over all. Repentance is rooted in the Jewish concept of changing one's focus in body, mind, soul and spirit; that is, with all of a person's being. Jeremiah, the prophet, echoed God's word to Israel promising restoration of the nation in a new covenant which Jesus referenced at a Passover celebration which Christians have renamed the Lord's Supper. Belief goes back to the everlasting Abrahamic Covenant in Genesis in that Abraham believed God to his credit as the father of many nations. When Jesus began his ministry, he did so as a Jewish rabbi recalling the Covenants from the Torah and the Prophets.

The gospel comes from the greatest command from the Torah in the familiar Shema prayer: "Love the Lord your God with all your heart and with all your soul and with all your strength."[1] The Levitical law includes loving one's neighbor as oneself. Jesus added loving one's enemies in his Sermon on the Mount. As in repentance, we see worship of God with one's total being. The gospel is holistic in its application to human beings. Salvation involves the body, mind, soul, and spirit.

The Gospels of Matthew, Mark, Luke, and John all have a statement from Jesus related to kingdom, repentance and belief. Matthew's words are similar to Mark's: "Repent, for the kingdom of heaven is near." Luke provides more detail about the kingdom in Jesus' manifesto of ministry which included preaching the good news to the poor, offering freedom to prisoners, restoring sight to the blind and releasing the oppressed. In another place Luke quotes Jesus as saying that he must preach the good news of the kingdom of God. Finally, the Apostle John records Jesus' conversation with Nathanael who believed Jesus was the son of God and the king of Israel because he actually saw Jesus. But at this event, Jesus spoke of all those who would believe without actually seeing him as the future church. In each case where Jesus calls his disciples, they appear to immediately change their mind, lifestyle, and follow. In response to Jesus' call, they do something. They don't kneel at the altar of their own spirituality. We now look at how this dynamic rooted in the Old Testament and typical of Jesus' call to his disciples characterizes all of Jesus' encounters with individuals where he commends their faith and pronounces their salvation.

We can safely say that being saved has no meaning or definition outside of repentance and belief. A biblical view of the gospel mandates a changed heart, mind, soul and spirit which is evidenced by a changed lifestyle. Generally, no example of Jesus recognizing a person's faith or speaking of them as saved appears to involve a unique spiritual experience.

The gospel of the kingdom, repentance, and belief is derived from the Old Testament. Consider the prophet Samuel's

---

1. Deuteronomy 6: 5.

conversation with Saul after the latter's disobedience using the animals from an enemy for religious sacrifice. Wouldn't this have been an efficient way to continue what God had prescribed for the nation? But Saul's apparent initiative violated God's command to completely destroy the enemy including their animals. Samuel's following statement shows how God prefers obedience to religious ritual. "Does the Lord delight in sacrifices as much as obeying the voice of the Lord. To obey is better than sacrifice?"[2] In other words living correctly according to God's word supersedes piety, even if they include doing the rituals the right way. Prophet Jeremiah mentions a new covenant in that God would in a unique way transfer the commands from Sinai in stone and plant his law in the minds and on the hearts of the people. Inner belief would result in behavioral change. This concept was new for Israel and represents movement toward the New Testament notion of individual salvation within the context of community. In New Testament language we would think of an encounter with Jesus which is fulfilled within the church. To restate, there can be no salvation for a person outside the church any more than life for an individual Israelite was granted when disconnected from her tribe or nation. Given this background of gospel and salvation from the Old Testament, we now explore encounters Jesus had with individuals to verify that a gospel based upon kingdom, repentance, and belief characterized Jesus' ministry. Jesus spoke of a person validating their faith by what they did in response. Typically, this was a testimony for what Jesus had done for them as a witness to others. In no case does Jesus affirm faith or grant salvation only because of a person's spiritual experience either before, during or after his encounter with them.

Jesus' time with Zacchaeus is the best New Testament example of the type of encounter where salvation and faith are determined by behavior and belief. Recall that Zacchaeus, the chief tax collector, has heard about Jesus and wants to see him. So he climbs up into a tree to look down to see if he can find him. Jesus invites himself over to his house and one of most hated men in Jericho

---

2. I Samuel 15: 22

welcomes Jesus with open arms. As he often did, Jesus has disrupted the religious and cultural norms of his time and is seen with a known sinner to the crowd's displeasure. It looks like the host was sitting waiting for Jesus to arrive when soon after Jesus darkens the door, Zacchaeus says, "Look, Lord! Here and now I give half of my possessions to the poor; if I've cheated anybody of anything, I will pay back four times the amount." This is one of most robust statements of repentance in the Bible. The chief tax collector not only promises to stop collecting high taxes consigning many to poverty, but also gives money back after selling half of what he owns and rewards those he cheated with a fourfold payback. But the money isn't the issue here. It's the immediacy of repentance. There is no mulling or debating like the rich man who deferred repentance by asking Jesus questions about who his neighbor was. Jesus' response is as immediate as Zacchaeus' repentance. Because he's repented, Jesus sees to it that Zacchaeus knows he's saved. There's no piety. Jesus observes behavior and then grants salvation. Notice Jesus' grace in affirming Zacchaeus' link to Abraham in spite of being hated by the community because of his vocation. This salvation event models how Jesus continued to grant salvation and grace to people based upon what he observed in their behavior. Let's take a look at another encounter Jesus had; this time with a Roman centurion in Matthew 8. The conversation between Jesus and the centurion reveals that the soldier has a paralyzed servant. Jesus heals the servant. What's remarkable about this encounter is what prompts Jesus to affirm the centurion's faith and belief. Jesus observes the soldier's humility. He hears faith in the centurion's belief that Jesus need only speak and his servant would be healed. He compared the military command-response dynamic to the power and authority Jesus had to heal the human body. This is what gets Jesus' attention. The issue was authority. That's what prompts Jesus to say that he hasn't found anyone in Israel with such great faith. Jesus sends him home and the servant is healed right away. The key element of the gospel at work in this event is belief in Jesus' authority to perform a healing. It's all about what the centurion believes about Jesus. It was quite radical for Jesus to commend the faith of a member of an occupying army over that of his own people. However, not all encounters with Jesus ended well.

Matthew records a conversation between a wealthy young man and Jesus where the repentance required for salvation is more than the man can tolerate. The seeking man assumes that he must do something to earn eternal life. Jesus suggests that he obey the commands. Here his true colors show up. His insincerity is revealed, for the man wants to select the commands he should obey. Jesus plays along and lists some commands all of which he has kept. Just when he feels he's going to receive eternal life, Jesus does what he always does and turns the tables. The repentance for his greed will be selling his possessions and giving to the poor. That way he'll be rich for eternity. This is more he can bear because it would mean he'd need to give away a lot. It's not that he'd be poor; it's that he can't countenance the thought of giving so much money away. The change is more than his lifestyle can bear. He leaves Jesus and goes away sad. One of the classic texts for validating one's faith by sharing the good news is recorded in the Apostle John's Gospel where we find Jesus talking with a Samaritan woman at a well. This event exemplifies how Jesus assigned salvation and affirmed a person's faith based upon the key elements of the gospel.

We note how sensitively Jesus cared for the woman in gently leading her to repentance. He identifies with their common need of thirst, engages her in theological conversation, and identifies himself as Messiah. She comes to faith and shares her story with the result that many in her village believe. This woman became an early evangelist leading many in her town to Christ. Her belief involved an intelligent response to the gospel. John records nothing about any inner experience of emotion in this Samaritan woman's conversion. Her life was changed in an encounter with Jesus. Jesus assigned forgiveness of sins to someone based upon the faith of others. Mark tells the story about a paralytic brought to Jesus by four of his friends on a stretcher. The lame man had to believe their decision to see Jesus for healing. Unlike Zacchaeus, we're told nothing about this man's sin. Jesus saw the faith of the friends in their behavior. They not only brought him but went to the trouble of letting him down through the roof. The man said nothing. Jesus healed his legs and forgave his sins. His spiritual need was met during a visible healing. The man walked away and many believed the gospel and praised God. We know nothing about the man's verbal response to salvation by grace through faith. This example models holistic salvation where both physical and spiritual needs are met. The gospel redeems the whole person.

A particularly poignant example of the gospel as kingdom, repentance and belief occurs in Jesus' conversation with a non-Jewish woman from Canaan. Jesus observes her faith after an awkward discussion of what appears to be his initial rejection of her request to heal her daughter. He seems to test whether her belief is real. She humbles herself before him. Her faith is the conduit for God's grace to her daughter. Jesus sees her behavior as evidence of her belief and her daughter's life was changed forever. Faith evidenced by behavior leads to an observable change in lifestyle. There is no other example in Scripture where the faith of a humble and ordinary individual is put through the refiner's fire. It offers hope for healing and salvation to anyone who has similar faith and belief in who Jesus is and what he can do.

There was a woman whose sins were forgiven by the faith Jesus observed as she moistened his feet with her tears of contrition and dried them with her hair. Everyone seemed to know her as the village sinner. Jesus saw evidence of her worshipful behavior toward him. She welcomed Jesus into Simon's home more than he did. This so-called sinful woman outshined the religious leaders within the village. She didn't deny her sin. She loved Jesus more since she was forgiven for more. She didn't say a word during the entire visit; she only wept displaying her admission of sin and desire to be forgiven. The gospel was done in this encounter as forgiveness is graciously granted by Jesus because of a person's faith evidenced in behavior. She worships Jesus as her Lord by anointing him. Our assumption is that this woman repented of her sinful behavior and continued to live in gratitude for what Jesus had done for her. Do I similarly realize what God has done for me with the same gratitude? Do you?

The Gospel

In sum, Matthew 25 ties Jesus' ministry together with a prediction of how God will judge people by faith in God and belief of the good news evidenced in repentant behavior. We first observe no mention of a conversion experience. Entrance in the kingdom, which was near but is now here, is granted based upon behavior toward others, not upon inner mystical experiences. The King is judging all the nations for entrance into his eternal kingdom. As in David's Psalm 23, the Father is a Shepherd-King separating sheep from goats. The sheep are blessed forever because they treated Jesus humanly on earth. Now they continue life eternal in the kingdom of God. The goats are cursed forever into an eternity which does not include the presence of God. They did not treat Jesus humanly on earth. The emergent question is obvious. When was the one who fed thousands of people and cooked breakfast for his followers, ever hungry? When was he thirsty, a stranger, without proper clothing, or ill? When, of all things, was Jesus a criminal behind bars? There is nothing religious here. This isn't liturgical worship of God. It's not Bible study or sharing one's faith with a non-believer. It is meeting Jesus of Nazareth's human needs. There's another aspect—how does meeting human need get you into heaven? How is this event a gospel of the kingdom, repentance, and belief? Jesus injects the provocative idea that *he* is that hungry, thirsty and imprisoned person. To treat people with all those needs symbolic of poverty and marginalization is to treat the Second Person of the Trinity that way. When you work in a local pantry and people line up for their bag of food for the week, you are giving Jesus food. When you invite a complete stranger from the highways and byways to your Thanksgiving table, you've invited Jesus. So this is what Jesus meant when he talked about a kingdom represented by people who've repented and believed in who Jesus is and what he did to save them. They demonstrated their faith by feeding the poor. That's the gospel. The bad news is the sin of goats headed toward eternal absence from God. No universalism here. No, we're not all going to make it. The clarity of this event flies in the face of today's postmodern and anti-Christian culture. The King reminds us of what we didn't do. "Lord, forgive us for what we have left undone." Luther would have us believe that Jesus walks the earth incognito as a beggar. He must have read Matthew 25. This text summarizes what Jesus said to begin his ministry in Luke 4 when he read the Old Testament lesson for the day from Isaiah 61. In these two texts we see how the gospel has Hebrew roots. The gospel is Jewish. Luke quotes Jesus as saying the following: "The Spirit of the Lord is upon me because he has anointed me to preach good news to the poor. He has sent me to proclaim freedom for the prisoners and recovery of sight for the blind, to release the oppressed, to proclaim the year of the Lord's favor."[3] Now we see what he meant when he talked about how the prophet's prediction was fulfilled on that historic Sabbath day in Nazareth.

Luke 4 is the introduction and Matthew 25 is the summary of Jesus' ministry on earth. As he said to the Pharisees at the through-the-roof event, healing and forgiving go hand in hand. Human beings are persons integrated in body, mind, soul, and spirit. This first chapter sets the stage for the rest of the book. We've defined the gospel as a collaboration of three elements—the kingdom, repentance, and belief derived from Jesus' words:

"The kingdom is near, repent, and believe the good news." We've noted that the gospel is rooted in Hebrew thought which includes the Shema prayer to love the Lord with all one's heart, mind and soul. We've discussed several examples of how Jesus assigned salvation to several different types of people. Finally, we've observed how Jesus equates himself with the poor as a criterion for entrance into heaven. We now turn our attention to the church where salvation for humanity is consummated within a community of persons who love God with all their body, mind, soul, and spirit and their neighbors as themselves.

---

3. Luke 4:18–19.

Chapter 2

The Church

THE GOSPEL AND THE CHURCH go hand in hand. The gospel is proclaimed by the church. The process of a person's salvation is incomplete until she is an active participant in a local community of believers; that is, the church. There is no salvation outside the church. In this chapter we will define the church from Jesus' own mouth recorded in Scripture. It begins that Christian tradition handed down over time.

Jesus speaks more about the kingdom than the church. Historically, the church has been viewed as "the already but not yet" kingdom of God. The church ushers in the kingdom. Just three verses record Jesus' mention of the church in the Gospel according to Matthew 16:18, 18:17, and 18:20.

In Matthew 16: 18 Jesus speaks of building his church on Peter, the rock. He forecasts that the powers of death will never prevail against the church. This is a promise on which the church can count through whatever persecution it faces. Jesus' first statement has two popular interpretations. The Catholic tradition has translated Jesus' words to mean that Peter establishes a church office of leadership commonly known as the pope. Apostolic succession is established to maintain a continuing presence of papal leadership. Non-Catholic Christian traditions, Orthodox and Protestant, establish church leadership without one man as leader who speaks for the church as a direct descendant of Peter. The non-Catholic interpretation looks back to verse sixteen and equates *rock* with Peter's confession that Christ is the Messiah, the Son of the living God. Jesus builds his church with those who share Peter's confession that Jesus is the Messiah. We agree with this second interpretation based upon other Scripture about the church. Peter preaches the first sermon where thousands come to faith. Along with Paul, he believes that the Gentiles as well as the Jewish people constitute the church based upon their confession that Jesus is Lord. There is no biblical evidence that Peter held a superior position to the other disciples, nor does Peter ever claim to hold so singular an office in the church. Rather, in his letters he speaks of the priesthood of all believers. Scripturally, there is no reason to believe that Peter saw himself as anything other than one of the twelve original apostles. The Bible never speaks of him as a father of the church. That would be God.

In Matthew 18:17 the church's role is to reconcile relational conflict. Ideally, an offended person goes to someone who has offended her and confronts them with the offence. When confronted the offending party confesses and the offended person grants forgiveness. That's how it's supposed to happen. If not, an offended person is instructed to bring another and confront the offending party. Should that not resolve the issue the unwilling person must be confronted by the church to hopefully end the conflict. The last reference to the church in Matthew 18: 20 implies that Jesus is present even among only two or three gathered in his name.

Other New Testament authors support the interpretation about the rock being Peter's confession of faith, not himself personally. Luke speaks of Jesus as a cornerstone. Similarly, the Apostle Paul speaks of Jesus Christ as the only foundation of the church when writing to the Corinthian congregation. These two texts hearken back to Jesus' teaching about how wise builders construct their houses on rocks, not on sand. Finally, Paul reflects on Luke's use of cornerstone imagery in Ephesians 2:19–22. Here he uses a similar metaphor to describe the church. First, he combines a foundation of apostles and prophets with Christ as the all-important cornerstone without which the structure would crumble. That structure is a temple of God, the church, cemented together by the Holy Spirit.

To summarize, the texts in Matthew where Jesus speaks of the church identify him as the foundation of the church verified by several other New Testament authors. Jesus is the founder of the church. Peter is one of the living stones in its apostolic foundation. No biblical basis for one person to assume infallible powers for the church in the name of Jesus Christ exists.

The Apostle Paul takes Jesus' "This is my body" from the Lord's Supper and names the church as the body of Christ. The Eucharist is the central event of the Christian church. Catholic, Orthodox and Protestant churches all celebrate the body and blood of Christ for the forgiveness of sins. The Apostle Paul names the Eucharist as the liturgical event which defines the church especially evident in his Corinthian correspondence. In chapters eleven and twelve of his first letter he speaks of the church as Christ's body using the human body as an illustration. Along with its healthy function as a harmoniously integrated organism, the body of Christ includes specific spiritual offices, gifts and functions: apostles, prophets [preachers], teachers, miracle-workers, healers, leaders, and helpers. All functions and gifts offer spiritual nutrition to the body of Christ. The Holy Spirit is the giver of all functions and gifts. The giver is more important than the gifts. It's Christ's body, not ours. In another place, Paul speaks of how a husband should care for his wife just as Christ nourishes and cares for his church. Finally, Paul goes to the extent of connecting his personal suffering on behalf of the church, Christ's body. He certainly endured much bodily pain throughout his ministry. Any pain endured on behalf of the church is redemptive. Bonhoeffer says that the church edifies itself by participating with Christ in his sufferings.

From the Catholic tradition we have a rich example of the church's origin as the blood and water flowing from Jesus' lacerated side. Physically this indicated that he was near death. Spiritually it's a profound example of the two key sacraments of the church: the shedding of his blood for sinners symbolized in the wine at

Eucharist and water baptism, our identification with Christ in both his death and resurrection. Here we have the church in direct contact with the death of Christ on the cross—a deeply rich symbol of the origin and life of the church intimately connected with Jesus of Nazareth's crucified body. Christ's resurrection, God's victory over death, brings life and power to the church through the presence of the Holy Spirit.

From both the Scripture and historic tradition we have the origin and life of the church vitally linked with the Eucharist as the unique celebration of the victory of God over sin for sinners on the cross. From Scripture and early tradition, we now consider how the early Creeds included the church as a significant element of the Christian faith.

Quite often in Scripture certain texts reflect that they may have been hymns sung by the early church. Philippians 2: 5–11 is one such text where succinct teaching on the humility and yielding of privilege characterized Jesus' cross. Another one-verse text in Paul's first letter to Timothy states the incarnation, angels, the universal church and the ascension in what may have been one stanza of a hymn. Hymns included in the canon of Scripture may have served as models of what later became creeds.[1] We now consider how earliest creeds speak of the church by reviewing the Apostle's Creed and the Nicene Creed.

The first doctrinal statement of the church is called the Apostle's Creed. Written in three articles to track with each member of the Trinity, it concludes with several stand-alone statements following the doctrine of the Holy Spirit. "[I believe] the holy catholic church, the communion of saints . . . " The church is holy. Only a church infused with the Holy Spirit of God can hope to measure up to this teaching. Similarly, a Christian must realize that his body is the temple of the Holy Spirit. The church is catholic, that is, it is universal across all nations, tribes, languages and cultures. The arrival of the Holy Spirit to launch the church at Pentecost in Acts 2 had Galilean Jews praising God in every known language. The church is a communion of saints. That is, it is a fellowship of

---

1. The word *creed* is derived from the Latin word *credo* meaning "I believe."

forgiven sinners-yet-saints. Though crafted much earlier, the first written Apostles' Creed appeared in a letter around 390AD.

The final version of the Nicene Creed, a more robust statement of belief, resulted from a church council held in 381AD. The Apostle's Creed had its origin in the Latin West while the Nicene Creed occurred in the Greek East. The Nicene Creed speaks of the church in this way: "I believe in *one holy catholic* and *apostolic* church. I acknowledge one baptism for the forgiveness of sins..." Note also the addition of *one* and *apostolic* as adjectives for the church. Here we have a robust view of the unity of the church as well as its continuity from early church leaders. So looking back at these two hallmark creeds of Christian doctrine, we note the significant place of the church. Having reviewed the creeds we move ahead in history to Martin Luther, one of the church's notable change-agents, and what has been called the Reformation which began in 1517.

Reformation denotes a re-shaping of the church involving the Word of God. This is Luther's chief contribution to the church which had forgotten the gospel of salvation by grace through faith. Luther resurrected the Scriptures as authoritative for matters of doctrine and practice.

According to Luther, the church must include the following seven elements to answer his question: Where can I find the people of God? He lists the following: Scripture, baptism, the altar [the Lord's Supper], office of the keys: confession and forgiveness in church discipline, ordination of pastors, worship in praise and prayer and the cross. Each one of these has biblical support and contributes to a robust theology of the church.

First, the Word of God was to be the authority for Christian doctrine and practice. The formal liturgy of the gathered church and obedience to Christ's commands as the scattered church in the world would be governed by biblical data. What the Bible mentioned, church leaders would implement in the church. Along with the Eucharist, the sermon took on greater prominence in the liturgy. Word and Sacrament defined a church of the Reformation.

Second, baptism was defined as dying to sin followed by rising to new life in Christ. Water was used during the Reformation and sprinkling of an infant was carried over as the method from the Roman Catholic liturgy. Infants were baptized into the community of the church to be nurtured as future disciples of Christ. In other Reformation traditions, adults were baptized as a result of a later commitment to Jesus Christ as Lord. Scripture doesn't explicitly prescribe a method of baptism.

Third, Luther defined the Lord's Supper as the *real presence* of Jesus Christ, the host of the meal. The Roman Catholic Eucharist has defined it as a sacrifice made *to* God *by the church*. Luther reversed the notion of sacrifice to say that Eucharist was the thanksgiving to God *for* the sacrifice made *by Jesus Christ* on the cross. It was about what God did for us, not what we are doing for God. Thus, Luther's view of salvation of body, mind, soul and spirit was captured in the seminal Reformation phrase, *justification by grace through faith*.

Parenthetically, and beyond the scope of this book, we need to briefly address how Eucharist is viewed across the several church traditions and denominations. There are two issues. First, there's the age-old discussion from the sixteenth century as to what's actually happening to the bread and wine during Eucharist. We will not concern ourselves with this issue. Suffice it say, the conversation centers chemistry, mystical presence and symbolic memorial. Secondly, there's the concern about who is allowed to participate in Communion. Some churches open the Lord's Table without criteria to anyone in attendance. Others deny the body and blood of Christ to anyone who isn't a member of their tradition, denomination or local congregation. We note that Jesus stated nothing about who could or could not take the bread and wine who have been church that day. Of course, he knew everyone at that Passover meal and priests or pastor cannot possibly know the faith journey of all people in their service on any given Sunday. Nor are they responsible to do so. Luther opened the Table to those in attendance in the same manner as Jesus at the first celebration of the Lord's Supper. An entire church council was devoted to the issue of who should and who shouldn't administer the Sacrament. If the priest had a bad week spiritually, should he preside over the Lord's Supper the following Sunday? The conclusion was that the Lord's Supper, because Jesus is the host, is inherently pure and untainted separate from those who offer the elements, priest or lay people. Paul talks about unworthily taking the bread and wine, where he's talking about a self-centered participation without regard that this act with the body of Christ as church in mind. We limit our statement on this topic to this sentence: we assert that all who follow Jesus because they know their sins are forgiven through the cross *must* participate in Communion to continually recall the grace of God in Christ for their salvation.

Fourth, the office of the keys is unique language derived from the Matthew 18 text which speaks of *loosing* and *binding* sins according to confession and forgiveness. Here is the gospel at work. The church is a liberating force in the world. Based upon admission and confession of sin, Christ offers forgiveness. On the other hand, Christ cannot forgive unspoken and unconfessed sin. Thus, the believer remains bound and yet-to-be-liberated. Often the church must show its high regard for holiness and restoration in the discipline members for the sake of the entire body of Christ. The objective of church discipline is to bring a member back into full fellowship with the congregation. It is not punishment. It is not retribution, but restorative. Church discipline remains one of the most misunderstood, neglected, and needed functions of the church today.

Fifth, along with the Scripture, baptism, altar, and the keys, Luther spoke of ordaining pastors, praise and prayer, and the suffering endured by the church as it carries the cross. The formal certification and ordination of pastors and church leaders was important to Luther from his high regard for scholarship and shepherding skills among the pastors and leaders of the church.

Sixth, Luther had a high regard for worship in praise and prayer as vital to the church. So the aspects of the *Kyrie, Gloria, Credo, Sanctus, Agnus Dei* and *Benedictus* are represented in worship among many church traditions. The church is visible in its

Word-centered worship. The liturgy included recitation of the Lord's Prayer, the public and private teaching of catechism, and the singing of psalms, hymns and spiritual songs. Eucharist was celebrated every Sunday. Word and Sacrament characterized liturgy.

Seventh, the final criterion for the church was the cross. Luther developed an entire theology of the cross. He preached from Paul's letters that the message of the gospel was the crucified Christ. The cross of Christ was the basis for why the church might expect to suffer for its faith in the world, just as Christ himself had done. Luther would agree with the Catholic theology of the church originating from the lacerated side of Jesus from which flowed water and blood symbolizing baptism and Eucharist. Christ's suffering sacrifice is why Luther called Communion the altar. Christ took our place for us and on our behalf. In Colossians Paul talks about suffering on behalf of the church. Christ's cross is our model for how and why Christians suffer in the world. We hear more and more today about the murder of Christians around the world. Such persecution is foreign to us in the US, yet normative for Christians from the days of the early church.

In sum, Luther established seven criteria for knowing where the church exists and what it is. The church is where the Word is preached, where baptism and Communion are correctly administered, where church discipline exists in the confession and forgiveness of sin, where ordination and training of pastors as scholars and shepherds occur, where congregations sing praise and offer prayer to God and where the church takes up the cross and follows Jesus.

Considered a second generation reformer, John Calvin weighs in on the church. He states, "The church is our mother ... God has given marks to discern his children. These marks are the ministry of the Word and administration of the sacraments instituted by Christ. We must on no account forsake the church distinguished by such marks. Those who act otherwise are apostates, deserters of the truth and of the household of God, deniers of God and Christ ... "[2] Furthermore, Calvin addresses Luther's office of the keys

---

2. Calvin, *Institutes*, 671.

THE CHURCH

with a thorough analysis of New Testament churches which fell prey to sin either in doctrine or in behavior. The grace of forgiveness is available for everyone in all places at anytime.

The greatest theologian of the twentieth century was Karl Barth. In his voluminous *Church Dogmatics*, he speaks of the church as concretely visible. "The Church came into existence quite visibly in the calling of the twelve apostles . . . it developed visibly with the addition of the thousands on the day of Pentecost . . . The Church never has been and never is absolutely invisible."[3] Barth offers a thorough analysis of the four-fold description of the church as "one, holy, catholic, apostolic" from the Nicene Creed. All of which is to say that those theologians who help us grasp the essence of the church go back to Scripture and the Creeds. The authority of the Word implies the authority of the church in its proclamation of the gospel. The church's only foundation is Jesus Christ.

We conclude this discussion of the church by consulting Dietrich Bonhoeffer who resurrected Luther in the twentieth century. The essence of his ecclesiology may be found in four of his books: *Sanctorum Communio, Discipleship, Life Together,* and *Letters and Papers from Prison.*

In his doctoral dissertation regarding the church as a fellowship of believers, *Sanctorum Communio (The Communion of the Saints),* Bonhoeffer stated, "Christ exists *as* the church."[4] When doing theology, it's often the little words that make a huge difference. Note that he says *as,* not *in.* Why not "Christ exists *in* the church?" After all, isn't Christ in us as believers? Doesn't Scripture say "Christ in you the hope of glory?" What's the difference between *as* or *in*? Were the statement *in* the church that would mean that there is something in the church which is outside of Christ. In other words, if Christ were merely a subset of the church, then non-Christian elements could exist in the church. Can anything which is non-Christian be in the church? Of course not. All of what the church is pertains to Christ. All of who Christ is *must* be

---

3. Barth, *Church Dogmatics,* 650–725.
4. Bonhoeffer, *Sanctorum Communio,* 189.

true of the church. That is, Christ equals the church and the church equals Christ. Jesus Christ exists as the church.

In his first published book, *Discipleship*, Bonhoeffer said this about the church: "Christ is the new humanity."[5] At first glance, this sounds like another way to say that Christ exists as the church, with this difference—the element of new humanity. This derives from the important teaching of the church called the Incarnation, or "The Word became flesh and dwelt among us" from the first chapter of John's Gospel. That Jesus became human as a baby made God visible. We wouldn't have been able to see him unless he became flesh. Parenthetically, the acid test for true spirituality is the incarnation. That is, if you're questioning whether a spirit is of God, ask it if it believes that Jesus came in the flesh. If the spirit denies this, run the other way. If it says yes, you're on safe ground according to John's first letter.

Life Together is a classic little book on Christian community. It summarizes how Bonhoeffer trained Lutheran pastors in theology while they lived in community. He saw the need not only for scholarship, but also for learning how to live together as Christians. He thought that day-to-day living together in community would prepare pastors to shepherd the church and model community. Then they could effectively guide their churches in doing the same. He said this: "Whoever cannot be alone should be aware of community. Whoever cannot stand being in community should be aware of being alone."[6] What did he mean? In other words, the Christian in the church should find a way to avoid being lonely but discover how to be alone in a productive way. Such being alone may be viewed as spiritual preparation for worshiping together in community. This also implies that one is personally responsible for one's actions and not dependent on the community. Christians aren't to be in denial about their problems only to make others feel responsible for them. As members of the church-community, we are not to avoid ourselves. But the reverse is also true.

---

5. Bonhoeffer, *Discipleship*, 215.
6. Bonhoeffer, *Life Together*, 82.

The Church

Christians are called to a community of faith. As individuals we carry our own cross, but do so supported by the community of faith, the church. We are not alone when we die because on the judgement day we will be only one member of a great community of faith. So, only when we stand in community can we be alone and only as we stand alone can we live in community. According to Bonhoeffer, the church offers solitude and community.

Finally, Bonhoeffer wrote some of his most radical statements about the church while in prison during the last year of his life documented in *Letters and Papers from Prison*. "The church is the church only when it is for others."[7] Bonhoeffer's Christology speaks of Christ not only as our substitute on the cross, but also our vicarious representative. That is, Christ not only takes our place in a one-time event, but also constantly advocates on our behalf as our priest before the Father. As a result, since the church is his body, we, too, become vicarious representatives for our neighbor. In a way we become Christ for them. Or, as Luther would say, each member of the church becomes a little Christ for others. Just as Jesus Christ is the only real sacrament, we become living sacraments as crushed bread and poured out wine participating in the sufferings of Christ for the world. Bonhoeffer continually scolded the church for its ingrown fixation on itself. He bristled at the neglect of its advocacy for the Jewish people during the nightmare years of the Nazis. The church is only the church when it participates in the mission of God in the world that God loves.

In this chapter we have defined the church both biblically and theologically from Jesus' own words, the Creeds, Luther, Calvin, Barth and Bonhoeffer. These first two chapters have been about the gospel and the church. They set a solid foundation for the rest of the book. Now we get into the bad news of those spiritual forces out to destroy the gospel and the church. One of those subtle influences is Gnosticism. It is to that nemesis of Christianity that we now turn our attention.

---

7. Bonhoeffer, *Letters and Papers from Prison*, 503.

Chapter 3

Gnosticism and Christianity

IN THE FIRST TWO CHAPTERS we've defined both the gospel and the church, the essential message and core organism of the Christian faith. The objective of this chapter is to see how Gnosticism, an old heresy of the church, destroys the gospel and the church.

What is Gnosticism? According to Hans Jonas, Gnosticism is special knowledge of an elite and enlightened people from the second and third centuries.[1] It is transcendence by inner religious experience. Gnosticism sees people as guilty for the evil of the created world which has been made by an evil god. That is, anything material or visible is inherently evil. The human body is evil. But human beings possess an internal spark of divine essence, the god within them, which when activated by an outside Messenger of Light saves a person by helping them to escape their bodies. Gnosticism is a dualism. It always splits reality into two segments. For example, a person is evil yet has a touch of divinity. Persons are spirit and flesh. The spirit is good. Flesh is bad. Human beings are to pursue anything which is spiritual and deny anything which is physical.

---

1. Jonas, *The Gnostic Religion*, xiv.

Gnosticism and Christianity

1. Gnosticism may be summarized in the following five statements:
2. All matter is evil; only the spirit is good.
3. God is unknowable unless one's divine spark is enflamed.
4. The Creator is an evil god who made an evil world.
5. Sin is the lack of special knowledge needed to escape one's body to become spiritual.
6. Salvation is direct participation with the good God.

Gnosticism pits matter against spirit. Christianity is a unity of matter and spirit. Gnosticism splits reality. Christianity integrates reality as a whole. Gnosticism denies God; Christianity worships God as God. Gnosticism demeans the human body. Christianity embraces the human body as God's creation in his image. Gnosticism separates a divine spark and the evil flesh of a human being. Christianity addresses a human being as an integration of flesh, mind, spirit and soul. Gnosticism generates special types of people with private special knowledge. Christianity is for all people in the public proclamation that salvation is found in no other name than Jesus Christ.

To assess Gnosticism's impact upon Christianity, we first consider how it undercuts the gospel. The gospel is a message of salvation for human beings created by the only God, who is good. God created human beings in his own image. Evil is defined by a spiritual being opposed to God called Satan, the source of evil in the universe. Human beings aren't essentially evil, but have been tainted by Satan and live out of harmony with God, who only intended that they know him. Evil is associated with knowledge because the story of Adam and Eve in a garden included a warning against eating of a Tree of the Knowledge of Good and Evil. But they did and sin entered the world to infect the good they had by being created in God's image. Without the intervention of a crucified Christ on the cross, there is no hope that our double-minded existence can become a singularly holy participation with God and his agenda for the world.

Note how the language and catefories of Gnosticism deceitfully parallel the gospel. First, Gnosticism perverts Creation as a good by calling it evil. What God consistently called good as found in Genesis, Gnosticism called evil. Who God created in his own image as good designed to know only him, Gnosticism calls evil since all flesh is evil. According to the gospel, the essence of evil is knowledge never intended by God; thus, the warning in the garden against eating the fruit from a Tree of the *Knowledge* of Good and Evil. God is all about giving us life; and giving life more abundantly. The gospel is life-giving. Gnosticism is death-giving.

Salvation from the evil inherited from Adam and Eve requires an intervention, just like all dysfunctional behavior. The gospel offers power over the sin of trying to be divine by not allowing God to be God. According to the gospel, original sin is trying to be like God. This is Satan's evil desire for all human beings. Here is where Gnosticism destroys the gospel by turning it on its head and offering an evil as a good. Gnosticism, a religion of redemption,[2] proposes salvation by activating the spark of divinity within oneself. The gospel never speaks of an inner divinity of the person. The image of God is not a statement of divinity, but expresses the sanctity of the human being. Gnosticism requires escaping one's evil body. The Holy Spirit indwells the body of a Christian as the temple of God. Knowledge within Christianity is valuable only to the extent that it leads someone to believe that Jesus Christ is Lord. Nowhere in Scripture is the Gospel portrayed as knowledge, even though it speaks of knowing the truth to be set free. This sounds Gnostic. It isn't. Because the truth is Jesus Christ, the good God who also claimed to be the way, the truth and the life. From John 14: 6 we have "I [Jesus] am the way, the truth, and the life, no one comes to the Father except through me." The Gospel is all about life, not knowledge. Gnosticism's offer of salvation through knowledge is vulnerable to self-flattery and spiritual pride which lead to death. Gnosticism can only offer knowledge. Christianity offers personal relationship with God through Jesus Christ.

---

2. Rudolph, *Gnosis*, 113.

Gnosticism and Christianity

The Gospel not only offers salvation through the bodily existence and death of Jesus Christ, but also new life because of his bodily resurrection. Gnosticism could never say this, for nothing positive or powerful could ever come from a bodily resurrection. This would be considered a contradiction. The Gospel is Jesus Christ's victory over sin on a cross and his victory over death by his bodily resurrection. This is why the Apostle's Creed speaks of the resurrection of the body. Scripture never speaks of a resurrection of the mind, soul, or spirit. Jesus didn't arrive on earth as a mind, soul, or spirit. The Word became flesh.

The Gospel offers salvation only through following Jesus as Lord, the center of one's life. No escape from one's body is ever mentioned in the Scripture. Obedience to the commands of Christ validates that one has been saved by what one does in observable behavior, not through inner religious experiences. Gnosticism's definition of salvation begins and ends with special knowledge. The Scripture nowhere speaks of a special brand of Christian with elite knowledge. Scripture speaks only of ordinary Christians who follow the Jesus of faith, who is the historical Christ.

To summarize how Gnosticism infects the gospel, we've seen how it destroys the good Creation and the human being created by the only God in the universe. God created human beings in his own image to know only him and the life he offers. We've noted that Gnosticism views salvation as escaping from one's evil body through a spirit-induced fanning of a spark of divine essence. We've noted how the gospel is holistic without Gnosticism's dualism. Finally, we've seen that the gospel is always offered to those who take up the cross of Jesus Christ and follow him as Lord. The Christian seeks to obey the commands of Christ. The Gnostic is "saved" only by an inner spiritual experience of knowledge with no reference to obedience to commands. According to Gnosticism the body is sinful and any use of the body is unavoidably sinful. So what Scriptures identify as sinful behavior, Gnosticism would call normal behavior. Gnosticism says, "Enjoy the sin! It's all your bad body can do!" Now that we've discussed how this heresy distorts the gospel, let's get into how Gnosticism perverts the church.

How does Gnosticism destroy the church? Let's recall some basics about the church. Paul calls it the body of Christ. From the wounded side of Jesus on the cross both water and blood flowed—a symbol of the church whose essential two sacraments are baptism and Eucharist. Luther reminded us that a clear link exists between "This is my body, this is my blood" and the church. To answer the above question, we now add another component of Christian theology which is subverted by Gnosticism—a theology of the body.

The human body has been created in the image of God. We've already addressed this aspect of the Gospel. Christians are persons whose bodies have been redeemed; that is, brought back to the image of God through the bodily suffering of Jesus on the cross and his bodily resurrection from death. All aspects of the body are essentially linked to salvation. Which is to say, the idea of lost souls is Gnostic and doesn't include the body. Since Christians are commanded to love God with all our heart, soul, spirit, mind, and body, all these elements of human nature are saved through Christ. It is more than just lost souls who come to Jesus. The cross is salvific for all human beings created in God's image as persons integrated in body, mind, spirit, and soul.

A theology of the body impacts the ministry of the church community of recovering sinners. Physical healing is a clear component of the Gospel, since our bodies are saved along with our souls, spirits and minds. The gifts of healing and prayer are included in the Apostle Paul's long list of spiritual gifts given to the church by the Holy Spirit. Marriage, that sacred union between one man and one woman, is the analogy Paul uses to describe the intimate relationship Christ, as husband, has with his bride, the church. This analogy is appropriate since it is the most sacred human relationship among human beings. Marriage is defined from Genesis in terms of the body. First, marriage begins with physically leaving parents to live independently as husband and wife. Second, both husband and wife become one flesh through spiritual intimacy and sexual union. This union is both symbolic and expressive of their intimate relationship. When God is involved, weddings are conducted within a sanctuary of the church to symbolize the union of Christ with his church celebrated in the marriage of a woman and a man, as wife and husband. To the degree that Christianity is portrayed as only a religion of the spirit, it is Gnostic. As derived from Judaism, the Christian faith inherits a theology of the body.

When speaking of Jesus of Nazareth who is simultaneously Lord of all Creation we view him as one person with two natures human and divine. When combatting Gnosticism, it's important to emphasize that the only difference between Jesus' human nature and ours was that his didn't include sin. Jesus was unable to sin. The humanity of Jesus cannot be neglected. This fact is stressed by the Apostle John in one of his letters to the church when Gnosticism was raising its ugly head and beginning to plague the church late in the first century. John offered a simple test of the spirits: ask if it believes that Jesus came in the flesh. Gnosticism would insist on the impossibility of Jesus being fleshly. John insists that Jesus, the Word, became flesh. In this same letter John concludes with a command to stay away from idols. Idols need not be wooden or stone images. They can be concepts and ideas. Gnosticism is a conceptual idol. It commands nothing. It does not and cannot offer life. From the Torah, we have a command in Deuteronomy 30, "love the Lord your God, walk in his ways and keep his commands... then you will live... I have set before you life and death, blessings and curses. Now choose life..." Such a choice is a choice for life whose body, mind, soul, and spirit are nurtured within a community of believers, the church.

Finally, a healthy person is a coherently integrated system of body, mind, soul, and spirit. Christianity is a synergy of the physical, mental and spiritual categories. Here we focus on the physical. Who would have seen Jesus if he arrived on earth as a phantom? The Incarnation, the Word as flesh, is foundational to any understanding of the Christian faith. Since Jesus Christ is a special revelation of God, we may say that grace has been mediated through the tangible. Thomas believed only after he touched Jesus' wounds. John was quick to say in his letters that the apostles saw, heard and *touched with their hands* the risen Jesus. D. G. Hart reminds us that "The ordinary way that God saves is through the means of his

Word, read and preached, and visibly signified and sealed in the sacraments with the enlivening work of the Spirit." In other words, God instituted forms to mediate grace through the senses of the human body.

To summarize, we've seen how calling the church the body of Christ challenges Gnosticism's demeaning of the body. Scripture nowhere calls the church the spirit of Christ or the mind of Christ. The Church is the body of Christ. The Apostle Paul insists that only a community of human beings created in God's image, Adam from dirt and Eve from a rib, can be associated with a God who came in the flesh to live among us. God's Son, Jesus Christ, is one person with two natures, human and divine. God thought so much of the human body that he came to earth as a human being. Not only that, he used the human being as a metaphor for his church, the body of Christ. That church is in constant need of re-shaping. In the next chapter we discuss the Reformation as a radical return to Scripture led by Martin Luther in the sixteenth century.

Chapter 4

The Reformation and Protestantism

IN THE FIRST THREE CHAPTERS we've defined and described the gospel, the church and Gnosticism. In the next several chapters we will analyze how Evangelicalism has evolved over its three-hundred year history. Our objective is to discuss the theological origin for *evangelical* as a term Luther used for the gospel. The term *evangelical* was first used for those persons who believed in the major tenets of the Reformation. As Evangelicals they believed that salvation was a gift from a loving God who gave his only Son that human beings may have eternal life. They were justified by grace through faith. They read their Bibles for the first time in German and finally understood the gospel as it was preached. They read the Scriptures devotionally to maintain their relationship as disciples of Jesus Christ. They studied the Bible to determine the major doctrines of the church. They understood that they were still sinners in need of the real presence of a forgiving Christ in weekly celebrations of the Eucharist. They were justified yet sinners. They were priests as representatives of God to one another and as advocates to God for one another *within the church*. They considered their savior, Lord, and brother.

A former Augustinian monk discovered intellectually and personally that salvation was a gift of grace through faith and not something money could buy. His anger toward a seemingly unjust

God was transformed to faith in a loving God. That monk was Martin Luther who started one of the most significant turning points in history. He left the withdrawn subculture of the monastery. He married and had several children with his wife Katharina. He based his radical teaching on the Scriptures which he interpreted into German from Latin. The newly-invented printing press spread his message throughout all of Germany in a matter of weeks and months. He never intended to leave the Catholic Church. He just wanted to re-shape the church by returning it to its Scriptural origins. He reinterpreted what really happens at the Communion table when the words, "This is my body, this is my blood" are spoken by the priest. His Catholic heritage taught him that the bread and wine were no longer bread and wine but actually became the body and blood of Jesus Christ. Luther maintained that Jesus Christ was really present as host of the Lord's Supper without requiring that bread no longer be bread nor wine no longer being wine. The issue was a matter of theology and chemistry. Bread or wine didn't need to change substantively for Christ to be present.

The new covenant about which Jesus spoke at that Passover celebration no longer had a lamb *on* the table, for the lamb was now *at* the table. This new covenant was sealed by Jesus' sacrificial death for sin and sinners. From then on only sacraments of bread and wine would be required on the table. Sacraments never lose their identity as ordinary items. They are simply assigned sacred value because of the context within which they are used. Luther understood all of this going back to the essential belief that even God became human. Jesus of Nazareth, a human being, was at the same time sacred as the Word who became flesh. He was the first sacrament. All subsequent sacraments are derived from Jesus the Christ. Since God became human, bread could convey his body and wine, his blood. The church was an ordinary assembly of people which is simultaneously a sacred community formed by the Holy Spirit. Luther remained within the church to reform it. Key to Luther's theology is his emphasis on the sacramental nature of

The Reformation and Protestantism

the Eucharist. Christians understood their re-entry into the world as "little Christs."

Martin Luther never uttered the term *Protestant* to define or describe his theological issues with the church of his time. *Protestant* didn't come into usage until 1529 at a meeting conducted by an emperor to solve the ongoing conflict about how princes could decide whether their provinces would remain Catholic or follow Reformation theology. *Protestant* does not refer to Luther's theological protest against indulgences, the pope or the monastery. Yes, he did protest the penitential financial system which deluded parishioners into thinking their sins were forgiven. But the term is about the followers of Luther who protested a power play Catholics made at a meeting called the Diet of Speyer to decide the politics of religion in German provinces. *Protestant* is a political, not a theological designation.

Protestantism is Gnostic. It sets up a dualism within Christianity. Neither Luther nor the other Reformers intended to start a new tradition of the church. Luther's disgust with religious pomp and popery didn't mean he no longer wanted to be Catholic. He didn't abandon the church in order to be a reformer. He was a reformer *within* the church not a runner *away from* the church. *Lutheran* is a term Luther despised. He challenged people to follow Christ not him. It was those now-identified Lutherans who proceeded to do exactly what Luther hoped they wouldn't—to start another tradition of Christianity. We've already seen this movie which includes myriads of Protestant denominations, non-denominations and brands—liberal and conservative.

The Reformation has roots in Luther's tower experience. Was the Reformation based upon one person's inner spiritual experience? No. Martin Luther never required that Jesus-followers have the experience he had in an Augustinian tower one day while reading Romans 1: 17 about the just living by faith. He *did* refer to it as feeling born again. It's important to get into what Luther *did* as a result of his born-again experience.

First, his experience did not catapult him from the church. In fact it informed a fresh theology of the church in line with

Scriptural guidelines. Secondly, Luther never demeaned reason even though he based his theology on the Scriptures as authority for faith and practice in the church. Were his born again experience authoritative over Scripture, he would have made it normative for all Christians. He didn't. His experience led him out of the monastic subculture into the public arena of the world. Luther's inner experience manifested itself in his key thoughts about Christian freedom. Contrary to Gnosticism, his experience led him into an appreciation for the humanity of the neighbor as a visible expression of his love for God. In *Freedom of the Christian* written in 1520, he said, "Christians live not in themselves but in Christ through faith and in their neighbor through love. By faith we are caught up beyond ourselves into God; by love we descend beneath ourselves into our neighbor." Gnosticism would never speak of being enlightened by being a "dutiful servant of all, subject to all." Luther maintains a holistic unity of love for God and love for the other which Gnosticism cannot abide with its self-centered narcissism. The issue here is not about spiritual experiences but acting in obedience to Christ's commands. It is not about being spiritual instead of religious. Gnosticism camps on a subjective experience of inner enlightenment. It disparages obedience to commands. Jesus demands obedience to his commands.

The Reformation of the church was a turning point in church history. Luther and the reformers resurrected the Word of God. That resurrection challenged a penitential system based upon payment of money to the church for one's salvation. The cathedrals in Europe are breath-taking. But they were funded by peasants who thought they were reducing the sentence of their relatives in Purgatory, a half-way house for the dead. It challenged the hierarchy of the church for its pomp rather than assuming rightful shepherding and leadership over the church. The presence of hierarchy wasn't the issue. Its corruption was. Luther never challenged structured leadership in the church. Scripture speaks of deacons, elders, bishops, apostles, pastors, teachers and evangelists. At the same time a clear tenet of the Reformation was the priesthood of all believers from Peter's letters to the church. Here we find a healthy balance between structured leadership and active laity both of whom participate in the life of the church. Finally, we mention briefly Luther's theology of the cross.

The Reformation gave the church a view of the cross which became a lens through which all Christians could see reality. Luther spoke of a theologian of the cross as one who called a thing what it is. That is, it viewed the cross as a non-religious tool of torture and death within the Roman culture. It was an object of shame within Judaism. It was foolish to have your god on a cross dying for sin. Culturally, criminals, not God, appeared on crosses. A theology of the cross looks at what's visible and says what it is. For example, the cross is a scandal for Luther since the Son of God is crucified like a criminal. But he doesn't shrink from this reality. Informed by the Apostle Paul in his first letter to the Corinthian church, he states that the message of the faith is *Christ crucified*. Here's Luther's basis for a theology of cross where truth may be hidden in the visible. A special revelation of Christ is hidden in the cross. The invisible truth of world redemption was hidden in the visible death of a criminal on a cross.

The visible cross containing the dying body of Jesus of Nazareth is literally the crux of the Christian faith. The cross has huge sacramental weight for the church. The sacraments of baptism and Eucharist are defined by the cross. In baptism the Christian dies to sin and becomes alive to Christ. In communion we ingest the body and blood of the crucified Christ. All of which is summed up in the phrase given to the church by the Reformation from Paul's letter to the Ephesians: "For by grace we are saved through faith . . . "[1] God's grace is the agent of our salvation; God-given faith is the medium. Salvation is a life-ling process which may begin with a decision to follow Christ, but must continue by participating in the body of Christ, the church.

To conclude, the Reformation provides a theology within which *evangelical* is defined. Protestantism is a non-theological term for the politics of religion in Germany. The Reformation is the last non-Gnostic expression of *evangelical*. Luther's use of this

---

1. Ephesians 2: 8.

word equated with the gospel became tainted by later reformers in the sixteenth century continuing to the present day. After the sixteenth century, disparate movements within Christianity and the church begin to create space for Evangelicalism. Among such movements are Puritanism and Pietism to which we now turn our attention.

Chapter 5

The Puritans and the Pietists

So far we've laid the foundation for the gospel, church and Gnosticism. In the last chapter we defined the Reformation and explored its use of *evangelical,* and pointed out the political nature of Protestantism. In this chapter we consider two movements which have contributed to Evangelicalism's ethos—Puritanism and Pietism. The earlier British Puritanism and later German Pietism both influenced Evangelicalism. According the recent scholarship, Pietism has had the greater impact.

The Puritans, as their title implies, were purists and members of the Church of England. As advocates of the Reformation, they observed that their church was too Catholic and sought to purify its doctrine and especially its piety. Puritans used *born again* as vocabulary for purity in spiritual conversion and devotion. Some Puritans required that to be truly born again one must have a dramatic inner experience followed by a prolonged period of introspection to be sure that one was saved. Puritans were among the first byproducts of Protestantism which influenced Evangelicalism. Puritanism's subjective piety was a direct input into how Evangelicalism defines one of its major tenets—conversion. Ironically, Evangelicalism tried to revive the spirituality of the church by leaving it. Puritans did the same thing when they arrived on the shores of the New World early in the seventeenth century. For

Puritans, ecclesiology was less about the Reformation and more about how to organize a church. Recall that Martin Luther's seven-point definition of the church was theological, not political. While the Reformation offered a fractured church a theological definition, Protestantism skewed with politics. The Puritans' autonomy in local church order and politics was heavily influenced by their dissent against the Church of England. There were theological implications to being a "Separatist" congregation. We'll see how this language of separation characterized Evangelicalism especially when thinking about being a special type of Christian.

The Puritans were Calvinists. Which is to say, they held to a deep belief in God's control of the universe including who would survive an election of being born again, and who wouldn't. That is, a sovereign God would pre-determine who would go to heaven and who would go to hell. Over time Puritans developed their own version of Calvin's reformed theology of conversion to suggest that one needed to have an authentic religious experience in order to be sure they were saved. What does an authentic religious experience look like? There can be no objective criteria to assess or validate experience since all experience is subjective. The only way to answer this key question was that everyone who said they felt saved needed to have the exact same experience. Those who could not articulate an inner spiritual experience remained part of Calvin's limited atonement. A doctrine which contradicted the Scriptural assertion that God willed that all should be saved.

So Puritans standardized on what defies an objective standard. Note the inherent contradiction related to making experience a criterion for salvation. Born again as a standardized experience carries with it the same self-contradictory implication be it Puritan or Evangelical. One person's experience cannot be compelling for another person's salvation. Puritans used mystical inner spirituality as proof of one's election by God for salvation. Theologically, we know that the Holy Spirit intervenes differently for every person. Spiritual experience is different for every person. Worse yet, not all spiritual experience makes Christ necessary. Stated differently, not all inner feelings of spiritual warmth are from God.

The Puritans and the Pietists

To summarize, English Puritanism had a direct influence upon European and American spirituality. A theme of individuality piety challenged the dead orthodoxy of church doctrine and polity. Every Sunday school student knows something about Puritan John Bunyan's *Pilgrim's Progress* written as one's spiritual journey to the City of God. Sixteenth century Puritan opposition to the Catholicism of the Church of England launched a similar movement of protest throughout Europe known as Pietism to which we now turn our attention.

The Reformation included a balance of personal devotion and doctrinal precision as informed by the Word of God and the Holy Spirit. Historically, a healthy church has always maintained a balance between Word and Spirit; that is, dogma and piety need not be opposed to one another. Note the Acts 2 account of the early church's attention to the teaching of the apostles along with prayer, spiritual community, and renewal. Reformation always refers to the Word. Revival always refers to the Holy Spirit. A balance of Word and Spirit are the norm for the church. We've seen with Puritanism an unhealthy shift away from a theology of the church favoring instead a focus on personal piety. That is, community gives way to individuality. Having taken a brief look at Puritanism, let's now get into Pietism.

German-based Pietism, though about a century later than Puritanism's beginning, had similar characteristics. Just as the Church of England appeared too Catholic for Puritans, Lutheran Orthodoxy seemed too dry and rigid for Pietists. The baby went out with the bath water; that is, a poor version of the church replaced the entire concept of the church. The church was traded off for personal spirituality. Small assemblies of piety replaced the community of the church as the location of God's presence among his people. Theology became subordinate to spirituality. Pietists viewed themselves as special types of Christians compared to those Christians who remained in the dry Lutheran church.

Philipp Spener (1635–1705) launched Pietism in Halle-Leipzig Germany around certain guiding principles. Devotional reading would be preferred to intellectual preaching. Spiritual lay people would be preferred to intellectually-trained pastors as leaders. Ironically, the Pietists advanced anti-intellectualism among Christians while simultaneously upholding the private and public use of Scriptures. Spener's ambiguity and confusion over personal transformation, individual spiritual rebirth and separatism from the church characterized Pietism in the same way that legalism and separation flavored Puritanism. Whether Puritan or Pietist, a Word-Spirit imbalance dominated each movement usually preferring inner experience to sound doctrine and teaching. However well-intentioned future leaders of the Pietist movement may have been, no one seemed to advocate a biblical alternative to the idea that experience had more authority than the Word of God. Pietism pushed the church down a slippery slope where Scripture as the sole authority for belief and practice was marginalized in practice though proclaimed in theory.

The church was demeaned. So-called practical Christianity and devotional piety were preferred to a unified community of believers. Johann Arndt's *True Christianity* had a wide influence on German Pietism. He, along with others, advocated moral reform to theological discussion. At its very core, Pietism displayed the characteristics of a protest that led to division within the church. How could a movement claiming to be inspired by the Holy Spirit divide a community of Christians? Here we see Gnosticism's ugly head rising to split reality setting up an unnecessary dualism between Word and Spirit, truth and devotion, and theology and ethics. The core issue differentiating Pietist Lutherans from Orthodox Lutherans was a heart-based holiness in one's lifestyle compared to orthodoxy theology. Clearly, pitting the Holy Spirit against theology cannot end happily. It didn't then and it doesn't now.

Puritanism and Pietism put a wedge into a holistic definition of a human beings created in God's image to love God with heart, soul, spirit, and mind. Each movement fell prey to Gnostic influence. Such an influence continued into Evangelicalism. Each movement defined itself as a reaction against something. Both movements required the existence of something they opposed. This begs the following question: If the Church of England didn't

The Puritans and the Pietists

seem so Catholic and the Lutheran Church so doctrinal, would Puritanism or Pietism have existed at all? One might even go so far as to say, that since Puritanism required a Church of England which it opposed, it was a parasite on its host. Similarly, since Pietism needed the orthodoxy of the Lutheran Church as its enemy, it too had a parasitic relationship with its host. We will carry this analogy into our discussion of Evangelicalism where its reaction against the church defined its existence. Neither Puritanism nor Pietism added any theology or spirituality which didn't already exist in the traditional historic church which both movements abandoned.

The gospel and the church are proactive. The gospel required a new Greek word for love: *agape*. No concept of self-sacrificial love existed within Greek-Roman culture. The gospel was original. The church was a unique assembly of people. Few understood how Jewish and Gentile people could love one another and gather together in worship given their respective cultural and religious backgrounds. The cross dismantled division between people and brought them together as one new humanity. Puritanism and Pietism gave rise to special types of Christians splitting the body of Christ. Evangelicalism would do the same.

We can now draw a solid line between Gnosticism's influence upon these two movements. Recall that the Gnostics boasted a special knowledge. Both the Puritans and Pietists claimed to experience a higher order of spirituality than merely ordinary Christians. Puritanism and Pietism fall under the Apostle's warning located in Colossians 2: 16–23. Here he lists "higher order spiritualties" related to self-abasement, worship of angels and visions. He challenges the spiritual pride and religious narcissism that result from pursuing the mere shadows of spirituality while neglecting the Word of God. Both the Puritans and the Pietists had their own way of going beyond the gospel and making commands out of issues for which there are no Scriptural mandates. To be fair, Spener advocated several of the key principles of the Reformation, especially that of the priesthood of all believers. As is often the case, his followers took his thoughts and pursued mysticism and elitism. We see today a similar repeat of church history where retreat from a decadent culture involves retreating into monasticism appears to be the answer. Spener's concern was moral purity. However, Christianity goes beyond fixing the morals and ethics of a society. Jesus never called his disciples to morality; which is different from asking them to be immoral. No statement of Jesus or any author of the New Testament mandates that Christian church is responsible for saving culture. Jesus came to seek and to save lost people, not deteriorating cultures.

Theologically, the answer to the pitfalls of Puritanism and Pietism is the Word who became an ordinary human being often challenging the religious purity and piety of his day. Jesus validated his divinity by breaking religious rules. He rejected the spiritual superiority of religious leaders. He fellowshipped with the impure. Jesus equated himself with the injustices of hunger, homelessness, illness and imprisonment to his disciples' surprise. Jesus was an ordinary Christian who sought only to do his Father's will. The Gospels speak of one who consistently opposed special types of religion. Jesus was not religious. He didn't advocate purity but appeared to be impure by the company he kept. Jesus didn't advocate piety as an end in itself but only as a quiet behind-the-scenes period of devotion intended to renew one's spirit for public ministry. When Jesus went off to meditate on the Word and pray to his Father, he didn't trumpet his spiritual experiences. His life was dedicated to a public witness to his Father's will. Jesus never required that his followers have the same devotional experiences of renewal as he did.

These two *isms* departed from the theological moorings of the Reformation and had more in common with a non-theological Protestantism. The Puritans were more interested in fixing a church than proclaiming an authentic gospel which required participation in the body of Christ, the church. Revivalism implied an individualism which turned the church to the Word of God. Spener meant to do the same, but his departure from the church led to the pitfalls we've described. While the Reformation tried to return a theologically-challenged church back to the gospel, a later

Pietism led to an extreme form of spirituality often resulting in spiritual perfectionism and religious pride. The emotional spirituality of these two movement inspired revivalism in America. Puritanism and Pietism led to mass revival meetings characterized by mystical inner experiences of emotion and feeling as well as by bizarre behavior. It is to these meetings called the Great Awakenings both in England and in the New World colonies of America that we now turn our attention.

Chapter 6

Cane Ridge and the Great Awakenings

IN THE LAST CHAPTER we investigated two major movements which informed Evangelicalism—Puritanism and Pietism. Each ideology required a unique experience as the proof of one's salvation.

In this chapter we continue to navigate other renewal movements designed to save lost souls. We'll first consider the First Great Awakening during the middle of the eighteenth century in America. Then we'll get into the unique Cane Ridge meeting in Kentucky in 1801 followed by the Second Great Awakening of the early nineteenth century. Once again we'll discover that these revival movements believed a born-again experience to be the litmus test of one's conversion. Was the Holy Spirit present and active in the so-called Great Awakenings? What is the biblical criteria evidencing authentic work of the Holy Spirit? What experience should a person have in order to be saved, if any? It's important to answer these questions as we get into the details of what actually occurred during these mass revivals.

The Great Awakenings preferred the spirit over the mind and body. Gnosticism accounts for this unnecessary dualism. How would someone worship the Lord in body, mind, soul, and spirit if salvation didn't involve the mind and the body? Mindlessness characterized the American Great Awakenings. Quite literally, they were a-musing; that is, not given to pondering or learning.

True, the church appeared spiritually dead in need of renewal because of so-called dry doctrine. But how could leaving the community of believers, the church, be a remedy led by the Holy Spirit? Mind versus spirit meant Word vs. Holy Spirit. Sadly no one saw this conflict for what it was and each side thought they were right. It's always that way when churches split. It's really a re-crucifying of the Son of God. Another way to state the issue is to pit Reformation against renewal. The early sixteenth century Reformation of the church centered on the Word of God. Luther's over-fifty-volume set of books is primarily exegesis and interpretation of the Scripture. His focus on the Scripture had to be Spirit-led because the Holy Spirit and the Word of God always work together. I repeat there can be no proclamation of God's Word without the aid of the Holy Spirit. There can be no work of the Holy Spirit which is absent from or contradicts the Word of God. So pitting Word against Spirit makes no sense. I would submit that the root causes of Puritanism and Pietism may be attributed to this unnecessary conflict between Word and Spirit. We now address revivalism's heavy influence upon Evangelicalism.

The First Great Awakening in America began in the 1730s and lasted for about ten years. The two names associated with this event were Jonathan Edwards and George Whitefield. The conflict within the church that catapulted this revival out of the church was a mind vs. spirit issue. In the case of this first awakening it would be a disdain for formal liturgy and an appreciation for an intensely individual sense of spiritual conviction and a commitment to personal purity and morality. Another way to put it would be pitting intellectual doctrine against emotional experience. The impact of this first American mass evangelistic event affected existing church members. It offered them an emotional outlet and enlivened their downcast spirits. Ironically, this movement split both Congregational and Presbyterian congregations. There were those within each denomination who supported the mass revivals and those who did not. Both Methodist and Baptist churches, already given to an informal liturgy, were strengthened. Persons who had a new birth experiences may or may not have joined local churches. The First Great Awakening fostered a transdenominational individual piety and devotion. A special type of Christian emerged without necessary participation within a Methodist, Presbyterian or Baptist congregation. Individual piety became the authority, not the church. So, if you belonged to all churches, you in effect belonged to no church. We'll later observe how this result of the great spiritual revivals impacted Evangelicalism. To be sure, there was salvation outside the church with the mass revival meetings. The issue was that what happened in a forest didn't necessarily translate into presence in a local church sanctuary. The "church" met in the woods. Its membership shifted with every meeting. No community occurred among people who sat in meetings night after night. What happened during the Great Awakenings appeared as a church. But wasn't.

The amorphous phenomenon of this undefined church created space for a piously devoted Christian to remain alone as a believer. Newly-converted Christians could have individual devotions, read their Bibles and piously kneel while praying without feeling any need to identify with the local church. Individual piety began the slippery slope of individual autonomy. A Christian could easily become vulnerable to self-righteousness and spiritual pride. Also, during the revivals, the marks of a Christian were not only a rebirth experience but also a second experience of personal assurance that one was really saved. There is no biblical mention of an initial conversion from a genuine encounter with the Holy Spirit which required another special spiritual event of assurance. This raises questions about the validity of the first born-again experience.

Biblically speaking, the marks of a Christian have little to do with emotional crisis experience. They are more in line with behavioral repentance producing a lifestyle based upon confessing and obeying Jesus as Lord. The second chapter of Acts gets into how the early church was known for observing the apostles' teaching, breaking bread and drinking wine, with prayer and praise in worship. This First Great Awakening followed the same line of thought as Puritanism and Pietism. There existed a de-emphasis on theology. The church was similarly marginalized. Overall, churches endured suffering from not adhering to the new theology of emotion. In *The Rise of Evangelicalism*, Mark Noll reminds us that for the last half of the eighteenth century no mass evangelist like Jonathan Edwards emerged. America had to wait for a unique response to moral decadence and a weakened church. That response occurred in one of the most uniquely religious meetings in American history—the Cane Ridge Revival.

Mark Galli has written about Cane Ridge and mentions a sign at a historic log cabin meeting house which reads, "*Cane Ridge Meeting House, Built by Presbyterians, 1791 Here Barton Stone began his ministry, 1796 Famous revival attended by pioneers of many faiths, 1801 Springfield Presbytery dissolved and "Christian church" launched, June 28, 1804.*" This sign is the paradigm of Christianity in America during and after the Great Awakenings. The Cane Ridge experience occurred in the wake of the First Great Awakening among a next generation of Christians none of whom attended Jonathan Edwards' revivals nor George Whitefield's first meetings. Note that a special church—a "Christian church"—was started. It replaced the Presbyterian church. Was the Presbyterian church not Christian? If it were, why change anything? If not, what did the Cane Ridge experience add to this new Christian church to make it Christian. The message on this sign would characterize Evangelicalism throughout it life. For just as Cane Ridge replaced a traditional historic Presbyterian church, Evangelicals would consider themselves unique types of Christians having had a bornagain experience which was superior to the dry-bones spirituality of the organized church. Christians without such an experience were viewed suspiciously. We observe that this sets up a dualism which is foreign to Scripture. The Bible nowhere speaks of special types of Christians based upon emotional conversion experience.

The Cane Ridge camp meeting celebrated Communion among over twenty-five thousand people. As the preaching occurred, people cried out to God for mercy and fell to the ground. There were stories about "visions and revelations, about voices heard in the night."[1] Religion was becoming experimental. The Gospel of repentance and belief was now based upon the story of a preacher's conversion experience. Emotional euphoria captivated a nation which was spiritually dry. There were few educated pastors to shepherd churches. Christianity needed a boost. The Cane Ridge meeting prompted future revivals that lasted for decades and yet also prompted many counterfeit revivals and cults. Let's look into this spiritual phenomenon. Of course, authentic conversions to Christ may have accompanied Cane Ridge along with many unexplained spiritual experiences where Christ isn't necessary.

The Presbyterians had planted a church in Cane Ridge ten years prior to the camp revival with Barton Stone as its pastor five years before the meeting. This was an ecumenical meeting attended not only by Presbyterians, but also by Methodists and Baptists. Each church grew in number. But the Cane Ridge meeting led to closing the Presbyterian congregation as previously mentioned. What was this new church? As in all prior spiritual movements theological and biblical doctrines were cast aside. The boundaries of defined local churches were blurred. Something very troublesome also occurred.

New non-Christian cults, Mormons and Jehovah's Witnesses, preached a so-called gospel along with Presbyterians, Methodists and Baptists. That is, counterfeit religious movements emerged from the Cane Ridge revival spawning a new religious phenomenon in America—a revivalism launching a spiritualism derived from a man-made gospel. Here is where we must interject the possibility of a Gnostic alternative to a theologically-sound gospel of a crucified Christ and a resurrected Lord. Why did the Presbyterian congregation at Cane Ridge feel led to close its doors in the wake of such so-called Spirit-led emotional conversions? Why weren't those new converts encouraged to attend the local Presbyterian church and grow its ministry in the area? Why weren't thriving local churches of all denominations "adding to their numbers those who were being saved" as Luke tells us in Acts? How could

---

1. Baker, *Evangelicalism and the Stone-Campbell Movement*, 98.

Cane Ridge and the Great Awakenings

non-Christian cults have been one of the results of a Holy Spirit-inspired event? Was the Cane Ridge event a work of the Holy Spirit? It certainly appeared to be another Pentecost. Was the swooning, head-jerking and dancing [unlike any self-respecting Presbyterian was used to in worship], evidence of God's presence? Our concern about Cane Ridge as the most talked about religious event in the United States in its day is whether it was an authentic work of God. Can God show up during high-pitched emotion? Yes. Is emotion necessary for authentic conversion? No. But are emotionalism, swooning, crying out to God, and dancing clear evidence of the Holy Spirit's working? The answer here returns us to the Gnostic-induced conflict of mind vs. spirit. How could cults with their non-biblical views of Jesus Christ be the result of preaching the cross? These questions beg other questions which focus on our earlier discussion of the criteria used to assess revivals. The so-called conversions at Cane Ridge are questionable as Spirit-led. At very best, the results of the Cane Ridge event appear to be a mixed blessing with confused outcomes. Pentecost launched a missionary movement throughout the known civilized world which left in its wake well-defined local congregations to which the Apostle Paul wrote letters of encouragement, challenge and instruction for living as disciples of Jesus Christ. The Methodists got more traction from Cane Ridge than either the Presbyterians the Baptists. Mass revivals bred the next revival until the large mass camp meetings died out. The emotion and hysteria of the next awakening had to be an improvement on the last meeting. The cry was, "may the next one be just like Cane Ridge." Let's now consider the next great spiritual mass event in America, the Second Great Awakening.

The Cane Ridge event had one significant difference from the First Great Awakening. The First Great Awakening did in part revive the church. Churchmen began to discuss revivals in terms how they are categorically the same as what should occur regularly in weekly local church services. The difference is only one of degree, not kind. This is a critical difference. Revivals are to be viewed only as heightened normal Christianity. Why shouldn't a local church regularly observe persons having life-changing encounters with Jesus Christ? Then, or now? The Holy Spirit hasn't changed since Pentecost. Healthy churches should not have been so reliant on mass revival meetings. New Christians should have been the normal result of local church ministry of the gospel. This gets us right into the Second Great Awakening of the early nineteenth century where things begin to change.

The Second Great Awakening was characterized by the unique preaching of Charles Finney, a Presbyterian minister who was the most sought-after preacher in the country and the best-known evangelist since George Whitefield.[2] Finney did not preach the gospel of the Bible. His view of sin, grace and the gospel was informed by the earlier N. W. Taylor who reduced the onus of sinfulness from character to actions; that is, people chose to be alienated from God without reference to a sinful nature they shared with all other human beings.[3] Essentially, the Second Great Awakening proclaimed a mongrel gospel devoid of the results of humanity's disobedience in the garden called the Fall. Without a fall from God's intended grace, Christ's death for sin is extraneous. Sins are the outward symptom of their root cause—a sin nature which corrupted the image of God. Only Christ's death and resurrection could atone for such a corruption. Finney's reliance on Taylor's false gospel would eventually lead Evangelicalism astray. Taylor didn't speak of the Holy Spirit as the cause for conversion. With Taylor followed by Charles Finney in his shadow, we have a non-biblical gospel preached by the poster child of the Second Great Awakening. Finney preached a gospel of democratic Christianity designed to cure the ills of an immoral society. He had no category for the New Testament church. What he wanted was a volunteer society rolling its sleeves up to stamp out the ethical and moral ills of America. Thus, his rightful outrage against slavery. However, the New Testament never required that the church transform a culture or rid an immoral society of its ills. Finney preached a non-biblical perfectionism foreign to the New Testament which

---

2. Fitzgerald, *The Evangelicals*, 35.
3. Noll, *America's God*, 171.

Cane Ridge and the Great Awakenings

never claimed that the cross of Jesus Christ removed sin. Charles Finney launched a movement away from the authentic regeneration of persons without Christ toward a more general view of a gospel which saved society. The task of genuine gospel preaching was to deepen the faith of Christians and encourage the church, not to correct a culture's ills. The impact of the church would result in a growing number of Christians who resisted a society's evil and over time see a reduction of sin's effects on a culture. Also, there is no biblical support for spiritual perfectionism. John reminded the church that it is self-deceived when it says it has no sin. The best any Christian might be is a recovering sinner, not a self-righteous person of grand spirituality.

In sum, Finney preached a gospel of Common Sense which attributed salvation to human decision and effort not to God's agency and grace on the cross of Jesus Christ. His message drifted from a concern for persons without Christ to a so-called gospel for improving morality and ethical behavior.

To briefly summarize this chapter's focus on Cane Ridge and the two so-called Great Awakenings, we find a drift away from the biblical preaching on sin, grace and the cross after Jonathan Edwards in the mid-seventeenth century, the Cane Ridge camp meeting and during the Second Great Awakening.

The first three chapters have laid a foundation of concepts to be addressed throughout the book—gospel, church and Gnosticism. In the last three chapters, we've begun a journey through church history to analyze key events which informed Evangelicalism including the Reformation, the Puritan and Pietist movements, Cane Ridge, and the Great Awakenings. Given this theological and historical background, we're now ready to define and describe Classic Evangelicalism.

Chapter 7

Classic Evangelicalism

NOW THAT WE HAVE a foundation from theology and history, we begin discussing the Evangelical movement itself. In this chapter we'll define Evangelicalism according to four key categories: *conversionism, Biblicism, crucicentrism,* and *activism* [1] using David Bebbington's formal terminology. We'll pay special attention to how Jesus, Paul, the Apostle's Creed, and Christian authors talk about conversion compared to Evangelicalism's reductionism of salvation to a one-time-fits-all experience.

Evangelicalism: Conversion, Scripture, the Cross, and Mission

Conversion

Evangel is the gospel. A born again experience is essential to being an Evangelical. Since *Evangelical* is derived from evangel, it's critical to be able to link being born again with the gospel. You can't. From our earlier discussion, we defined the gospel as kingdom, repentance, and belief. There is no mention of experience of any kind in the words Jesus used to launch his ministry. The gospel is what defines a Christian. Experience defines an Evangelical. Simply put,

---

1. Bebbington, *Evangelicalism in Modern Britain*, 5.

there is no statement in the entire New Testament which associates an inner experience of being born again with salvation through Jesus Christ. We begin by analyzing the only substantive text in Scripture which uses the idea of being born again from the familiar conversation between Jesus and Nicodemus located in the third chapter of the Apostle John's Gospel.

Born again is a mistranslation of John 3: 3 where Jesus says, "I tell you, no one can see the kingdom of God without being *born from above*." Traditional interpretations of Jesus' words above translate the Greek *born from above* as *born again*. *Born again* is not the same as *born from above*. Just as Nicodemus missed Jesus' point, so has Evangelicalism. The original language focuses on the agency of being saved. That is, it's about *who* causes one's salvation; not *how many* births one has. It's all about God doing the saving; not my experience of what he's accomplished. Later in the conversation, Jesus guarantees entrance into the kingdom of God by being *born of water and Spirit*. This involves both baptism and a supernatural intervention of the Holy Spirit. Finally, Jesus uses the phrase *born of the Spirit*. His reference to the Holy Spirit underscores that God is the agent of salvation. The difference in vocabulary is more than semantics. Christianity's theology of salvation is based upon the grace of God in Christ *from above by the Spirit*. Biblical salvation originates by its agent on earth, Jesus Christ. That said, we now consider what might be considered conversion experiences of well-known Jesus-followers; namely, the Apostle Paul, Martin Luther and John Wesley.

Everybody knows Saul-who-became-Paul's experience on his way to Damascus to throw Christians in jail. All of a sudden a light from heaven flashed around him and a voice asked why he was persecuting God. He answers his own question with the question, "Who are you, Lord?" Apparently, he knew it was Jesus' voice. Jesus identified himself and commanded him to continue on his trip to Damascus. Saul obeyed Jesus. His experience was physical. He was speechless. He went blind. He didn't eat or drink for three days. This was not a Cane Ridge experience. His story includes a man, Ananias, who has a vision and hears the Lord give him directions to a house where he will find Saul, who is praying! Not only that, Saul will know about Ananias because he's having an informative vision. Ananias knows all about Saul and obeys only after he's told that Saul is not the same person he was. Saul experiences two things: restored sight and being filled with the Holy Spirit when Ananias lays hands on him. Ananias then baptizes Saul, feeds him and he's restored to health and strength. The rest is a history of Saul's repentant life, his belief that Jesus is Messiah, and preaching in synagogues and churches all over the known world. His conversion is both individual and communal; that is, it involves him dramatically and the church. There is no way to speak of Saul's conversion outside of the church. His contact with the church begins with Ananias, a Christian brother, who is the church for Saul. You know, where two or three are gathered, Jesus is there. Saul will be in community with other Jesus followers for the rest of his life. He will be partners in mission with different believers. He will start churches and return to those same congregations to see how they're doing. His spiritual experience resulted in a new-found belief in Jesus as Lord in whose name he planted several churches.

Was Saul born again? Would you say he was born from above by water and the Spirit? There is no mention of born again either by him, Ananias or anyone. There is no indication that he made any decision to follow Jesus, for he needed to be led by others. He was totally dependent upon God's grace. He would proclaim the grace of God for salvation all over the world. Saul was born from above by water and the Spirit. He heard God's voice from heaven, he prayed to God while waiting for Ananias, he was baptized and filled with the Holy Spirit through Ananias. The validation of Saul's conversion was not evidenced by a spiritual experience, but by a radical change in his behavior. Jesus was his Lord. Saul, who imprisoned Christians was now Paul, who liberated people from sin by pointing them to Jesus, the Messiah. People noticed. People feared him at first. They were convinced, not by only by his testimony, but by his preaching and newly-discovered relationships with other Christians. All the criteria of the gospel were met in

Saul's conversion—the church [kingdom], repentance, and belief of the good news. Not to mention preaching the good news resulting not in life of pious experiences, but in new congregations of recovering sinners like himself. Martin Luther had a life-changing experience in his Augustinian monastery. He was reading his Bible Augustine's interpretation of Romans 1: 17: "For in the gospel the righteousness of God is revealed from faith to faith, as it is written, 'The righteous shall live by faith.' " It was written centuries earlier by Prophet Habakkuk who proclaimed the word of God to Judah prior to its captivity in Babylon. He argued with God first about why He was doing nothing about Judah's wickedness that disagreed with God's injustice of bringing in a pagan nation to destroy Jerusalem for their wickedness. When Luther read this text, he too had a debate going with God. He was an impeccable monk, yet continually found himself standing before a righteous God with a bad conscience about his sins. He hated God. The righteousness that he was to achieve by his own merits was the same righteousness that God used to punish sinners. This situation only deepened the dark night of his soul into emotional depression. Then while reading Romans 1: 17 again it dawned upon him that the righteousness he was unable to muster to appease an angry God of justice was given to him as a gift of God's grace and mercy through the cross of Jesus Christ. He said, "I felt myself to be reborn . . . " Scripture took on a new meaning for him. What does Luther teach us about being born again? What actually happened to Martin Luther when he read this text which launch one of the most important events in Western civilization—the Reformation? He claimed to have a reborn experience. What evidenced his experience as an authentic work of the Holy Spirit? His experience occurred while reading Scripture and altered his view of Scripture forever. Here we have a principle not to be neglected. No genuine work of the Holy Spirit occurs outside of the Word and nothing true about Scripture occurs without the intervention of the Holy Spirit. Evangelicals, as well as other Christians, haven't always understood this. There can be no question that his experience resulted in repentance; that is, in a change of mind leading to changed behavior. He left the monastery, not the church. He got married and had children. He railed against non-biblical traditions counter to the gospel. It almost cost him his life. It led to a translation of the Scripture into German which spread throughout the land quickly through the help of the printing press. There can be no doubt that Martin Luther's born again experience was an authentic work of God. His experience clearly met the criteria of the Gospel comprised of the kingdom, repentance and belief.

To do the gospel is to repent, believe, and become a member of God's kingdom. If conversion is to have anything to do with the gospel, it must involve the church. Sadly, Bebbington has excluded the church from his definition of Evangelicalism. But he's not totally at fault; for the movement left the church. And here's the key: Scripture never speaks of salvation or conversion without an explicit or implicit reference to the church. Paul wrote letters of encouragement, rebuke, and instruction only to churches. The Apostle John wrote seven letters to churches in Revelation. In this next section, we look into Scripture to observe the biblical basis for the assertion—omitted in Evangelicalism—that without participating in the body of Christ, the church, no one can claim to be saved.

The Apostle Paul's first letter to the church in Corinth clearly defines the unique message of the gospel. Not once did he speak of salvation through the death and resurrection of Jesus Christ as a born again experience. He simply states that our message is Christ crucified. The cross is the crux of the Gospel. The cross represents weakness and humility. It is scandalous. It is the price Christ pays for humanity's salvation. No other religion praises its leader for his death. Shortly after writing this letter, the Apostle Paul wrote a letter to the church in Rome around 57 AD.

In Romans 10: 9, 10 Paul defines salvation based upon verbal confession and sincere belief. Here he uses *confession* as agreement. " . . . if you confess with your mouth, 'Jesus is Lord,' and believe in your heart that God raised him from the dead, you will be saved." Note that the substance of one's verbal agreement is that Jesus is the Lord of the Universe. He didn't speak of salvation as a

CLASSIC EVANGELICALISM

confession that Jesus is *Savior*. Jesus *is* the Savior of the world, but he becomes one's Savior based upon a person's confession of Jesus Christ as Lord. This verbal confession implies obedience and taking up Christ's cross and following. Merely believing implies only accepting the fact with no suggestion of outward behavior. Recall that Jesus' first words about the gospel included *repent*. Lordship implies repentance. In a letter written about 60AD to the Ephesians, the Apostle Paul gets into an important aspect of the gospel.

In Ephesians 2:8-10, he specifies that salvation is offered because of what God does, not by what we do or feel. God's grace, not our effort, accomplished salvation for all humanity. Being born from above is just another way to say that God's saves. The undeserved act of a crucified God is the gracious and merciful basis for being born of the Spirit. The Spirit is God's *agent*. The faith God gives us to confess and to believe is God's *process*. Faith is the medium through which the Spirit helps us believe and live out the gospel. Nowhere in this seminal salvation text does the Apostle Paul speak of victory over sin or death in terms of an inner spiritual experience. The Gentile doctor and historian Luke records the details of the early church. In the few places where the New Testament mentions a personal conversion, he reiterates his earlier statement about confessing Jesus as Lord. The Holy Spirit accounts for being born from above supernaturally. A changed life, conversion, is what happens to the Christian. No Christian can convert herself by making a decision or by having an emotional experience. Deciding and feeling may accompany, but not cause, God's movement in a person's life. The evidence of one's conversion is a shift in attitude toward God, new belief, and obedient behavior.

Titus 3: 4-7 is a robust analysis of the gospel which incorporates much of what we've discussed above. It speaks of rebirth as a way to speak of salvation. It does so within the context of our earlier look at *born from above* in John's Gospel. Recall that there and now here, the issue is agency. Paul states that when the both the kindness, love and mercy of God appeared, he saved us. There's the agency—God. Grace now is communicated as kindness and love. It's all about who God is and what he does to accomplish our salvation. "He [God] saved us through the washing of rebirth and renewal by the Holy Spirit . . . " There's the agency of the Holy Spirit through whom the Christian is reborn and renewed. Unlike the mistranslated use of *born again* in John for *born from above*, there can be no question that the emphasis is on what God does, not on what type of inner spiritual experience a person has. Paul makes explicit use of his most familiar phrase regarding salvation, justified by grace, to cap off this theologically-packed discussion of redemption. By the way, justified by faith doesn't fully capture God's intervention in our dysfunctional lives. It's "justification by grace through faith," that Paul uses in Ephesians. *By grace* is agency; *through faith* is process. God's provides both the grace and faith.

It would be a few hundred years later that salvation would be documented as a doctrine of the Church in the Apostle's Creed. "I believe in Jesus Christ, God's only Son, our Lord . . . " It mentions the Lordship of Jesus Christ. Note the Creed doesn't say, "Jesus, our Savior." The focus is upon Jesus as Lord of all creation. He becomes our Savior when we confess him as Lord; not vice versa. "He suffered . . . was crucified, died and was buried; he descended to hell . . . the forgiveness of sins . . . " Here we have the victory over sin accomplished at the cross. "On the third day he rose again . . . " Here's the victory over death accomplished through Christ's resurrection. "I believe in the Holy Spirit" . . . .recall John's words quoting Jesus about being *born of the Spirit.* These are the words used in the first doctrinal statement of Christianity's core beliefs.

Early in church history, the following statement took on special meaning: *There is no salvation outside the church.* While this provocative statement does not explicitly appear in the New Testament, Jesus associated Peter's confession with building his church. In fact, this statement has its origin in Jesus' words about the gospel as kingdom, repentance and belief. Jesus links the kingdom and the gospel as we've stated earlier. The confusion lies in that some have taken it mean that only a particular Christian tradition, denomination or movement offers true salvation. We take it to mean that salvation is fulfilled by participation in a local congregation as

CLASSIC EVANGELICALISM

evidence that one is born from above by the Holy Spirit. Salvation implies community just as the first people of God, Israel, were a nation of tribes. Just as no Jewish person would ever practice her faith separate from her synagogue, no Christian can follow Jesus Christ as Lord outside of the church, a community of the body of Christ. So we can say that the process of being saved, or working out one's salvation, occurs and is fulfilled in the church. No lone rangers for Jesus are ever mentioned in the New Testament. Now that we've looked at Scripture and the Apostle's Creed to link salvation to the church, we get into what respected Christian authors have said about experience as it relates to salvation and conversion.

J.I. Packer in *Evangelicals Today* offers a solemn warning regarding Evangelicalism and its drift from the Reformation and Luther's gospel which focused on the hopelessness of salvation without the grace of Christ. His concern relates to the age-old confusion exemplified in the phrase justified by faith. The accurate way to state this biblically is justified *by grace* through faith. This is more than semantics. Were we saved by faith only, we could take some credit for our salvation. We placed our faith in Christ and we're saved, we might be tempted to think. But even the faith we have is part of the gift of God's grace. The emphasis must be on grace which is God's act. God is the agent of our salvation. We're guided by the Holy Spirit to place our God-given faith in the necessary and sufficient work of Christ on the cross. Packer finds elements of self-help salvation among Evangelicals who disregard their total helplessness to do anything to save themselves, even a decision constitutes such self-help. There isn't a person who's ever been saved because of their decision to accept Jesus as their personal Savior from sin. A person is saved by being reconciled to God by grace through faith. Precision of words is crucial here. Decisions and experiences save no one. They are merely aspects of God-given faith through which grace is extended to us. It's all about God, not about us.

Frances Fitzgerald discusses revival meetings where the emphasis was on the experience of a new birth, rather than on any exercise of reason or knowledge of doctrine. Sydney Ahlstrom described conversion during Edward's conversion experience as "genuinely new kind of vision of God's glory."[2] Ahlstrom points out how Edwards validated revivalist experiences in that they resulted in acts of charitable behavior. That said, Jonathan Edwards uniquely embodied both the genuine spiritual experience of true conversion, repentant behavior on behalf of others. Most significantly, Edwards never abandoned the basic Scriptural doctrines of original sin and redemption through the cross of Christ. Finally, Mark Noll speaks of how "authentic Christian experience" would take precedence over church-order and in later forms of Evangelicalism distort "inherited traditions of Reformation Protestantism"[3] leading to a trivialization of the gospel. This statement merits more analysis than we can offer here. Ironically, Evangelicalism claims Scripture as its primary authority in *theory*, but elevates experience as its primary authority in *practice*. Eventually, to its demise, such elevation of experience accompanied by a marginalization of Scripture would sound the death knell for Evangelicalism. We now consider Scripture's role in defining Evangelicalism.

Scripture

Sola Scriptura is without question what Evangelicals would require when defining themselves. However, any ordinary Christian would make the same claim. To its detriment what is unique to an Evangelical view of Scripture is how debates over how to express the Bible's authority rather than the more important discussion of *what* the Bible says about living a transformed life. Without getting bogged down in this dialogue, suffice it to say we're talking here about how the heated debate over inerrancy reduced Evangelicalism's credibility. Scripture only claims to be inspired, not that it's inerrant. In *No Place for Truth*, David Wells said this—"while the nature of the Bible was being debated, the Bible itself was quietly falling into disuse in the church."

---

2. Ahlstrom, *Religious History of the American People*, 295–313.
3. Noll, *Rise of Evangelicalism*, 292–93.

Classic Evangelicalism

Views about Scripture vary within mainline Protestantism. This, of course, is one of the key concepts which separates Evangelicals from liberal Protestants. On the other hand, Catholics are more and more using *evangelical* to describe themselves as George Weigel says in *Evangelical Catholicism*. Theologian Max Stackhouse states that because Evangelicalism possesses no structured authoritative body, it insists on the liberty for individual Christians to interpret the Bible for themselves informed by Luther's priesthood of all believers. Individual interpretation of the Bible has opened the door for an increased conflict and confusion within Evangelicalism. At its best, Evangelicalism makes strong claims that Scripture is authoritative and normative for matters of belief and practice. Ironically, those matters of belief and practice are addressed to the church from which Evangelicalism has removed itself. In *Scripture as Real Presence*, theologian Hans Boersma sums it up this way: "The Bible's place is not the academy, but the Church. My advice is this: Follow the Church's tradition in looking for Christ in the Scriptures . . . keep in mind why you came to this text. It was to know Christ Jesus . . . Don't be pulled out of the text . . . Stick to the text, look for Christ . . . the treasure is there. You'll discover you're one of its gems." Bebbington names *crucicentrism*, the cross at the center, as a third component. The substitutionary sacrifice of Jesus Christ for sin is crucial to any definition of Evangelicalism.

The Cross

Just as the cross on which Jesus was nailed was in the center of three crosses, so also is the cross central to Christianity and Evangelicalism.

As the Apostle Paul insists, the message of our faith is *Christ crucified*. It sets Christianity apart from all other world religions. No other religion worships its founder because he chose to die. Only Jesus was our substitute for the death we deserved as sinners condemned to eternal separation from God. That's hell both on earth and in the Apostle John's Apocalypse, a lake of unquenchable fire. From Bonhoeffer we find another aspect of the cross. Jesus is our vicarious representative. That is, he dies not only *instead of us*, but *for us, on our behalf* as our everlasting defense attorney (our advocate) to the Father. The crucified Christ is both our substitute and vicarious priest. To repeat, he dies *instead of us* and simultaneously *on our behalf.* Evangelicalism has typically limited itself to what's called a substitutionary atonement of the cross. Jesus is our replacement only. Evangelicalism can't offer day to day discipleship if from a cross where God *only* takes our place. Justification by grace through faith is a living phrase for Jesus' ongoing relationship with the Christian. Evangelicalism's lack of theological depth would hear Luther's theology of the cross and Bonhoeffer's echo of Luther as new language. Its reductionism of theology indicts Evangelicalism's bumper-sticker articulation of the gospel.

Bonhoeffer's vicarious atonement extends Jesus' role as our continuing advocate, our intercessor and priest, before the throne of God. Jesus as our replacement stops with the historic event and ushers us to heaven at death. Jesus as our vicar and priest brings God alongside us every moment of every day as one who is present as the Holy Spirit. The issue here is the *both-and* which resolves the problem of the *either-or* when confronted with a theological conflict. So Luther's theology of the cross revived by Bonhoeffer's church of the cross offers the Christ who takes our place *and* comes alongside us. The once-for-all act of the cross which removes eternal death for us also makes the power over sin accessible through the Holy Spirit. At the cross Jesus provides victory over sin—victory over sin's penalty and victory over sin's power. Jesus' victory over sin's penalty arrives in his role as our substitute. Jesus' victory over sin's power comes in his role as our priest. Atonement, being reconciled to God, is both substitutionary and vicarious. None of this is possible without the scandalously occupied cross of Christ which is humanly foolish and weak, yet, ironically God's unusual idea for how to save humanity. Having considered conversion/experience, Scripture, and the cross, we now get into the fourth component for defining Evangelicalism—mission.

Mission

Here we replace Bebbington's *activism* with the more biblical term *mission*. We do so because he defines activism as "the expression of gospel in effort." So defined, activism is more sociological than theological. Mission, on the other hand, is inherently theological being derived from "sent" buttressed by Jesus' words, "As the Father has sent me, so send I you." The so-called Great Commission from Matthew cannot be reduced to activism, but is better defined by the theological *Missio Dei* [the mission of God]. It is the mission of God on earth that matters, not even the mission of the church. *Missio Dei* is all about going, gospel-proclaiming, disciple-making, baptizing and teaching the Scripture around the world to every tribe, culture, tongue and nation. So we find Bebbingtion's reduction of mission to activism missing the mark.

That said, the issues of social justice, about which Evangelicalism finally became aware in the 1980s, are part of the gospel's ministry to the body integrated with the soul and spirit. Ironically, Evangelicalism's critique of liberalism's "social gospel" in the 1930s and beyond vanished as it embraced its own version of a gospel of justice, compassion and mercy. A holistic gospel was all that Jesus ever proclaimed. Jesus ministered to persons defined by an integration of body, mind and spirit. Jesus didn't point out the homeless man sleeping on a park bench. Jesus said he *was* the homeless man sleeping on the park bench. Jesus doesn't let us off the hook by merely visiting prisoners. Jesus *is* the prisoner we visit when we talk through the bars to an inmate. The liberal arm of Christianity saw this aspect of social justice long before Evangelicals, even though a gospel of redemption of the spirit and soul was lacking within mainline Protestant churches throughout the twentieth century.

Finally, we note that while determining a theology doesn't include mission, Evangelicalism cannot be defined without mission. Evangelism is proclaiming and saying the good news. It is evangelical to do so. Even on its worst day in America over the centuries, Evangelicalism is to be credited with attempting to spread the tidings all around that Jesus saves. Evangelicalism is also to be credited by adding mission as a component to theological development. To summarize, this chapter began with a brief overview of Evangelicalism's history beginning with the Reformation to the eighteenth century where the movement came into its own. Then we analyzed David Bebbington's four-part definition of Evangelicalism: conversion, Bible, cross and activism (mission). We focused upon conversion to discover the undue stress Evangelicalism assigns to experience its major component compared to Jesus' definition of his ministry as kingdom, repentance and belief and how he spoke to individuals about salvation without the necessity of an inner spiritual experience. In theory, Evangelicalism assigns ultimate authority to Scripture; in practice, it's all about experience. We looked into Paul's theology of salvation and consulted respected authors on the minimal role experience plays in authentic conversion. A concise definition of Evangelicalism is hampered by its amorphous qualities. There's a reason for all this—Gnosticism. In the next chapter we show that Evangelicalism is at best vulnerable to Gnostic influence or at worst a modern-day emanation of Gnosticism itself.

Chapter 8

Evangelicalism and Gnosticism

IN THE LAST CHAPTER we defined Evangelicalism with experience as its *sine qua non*. In this chapter we'll propose that Evangelicalism is at best vulnerable to Gnosticism and at worst a type of Gnosticism itself. There are two areas of concern: first, the authority given to inner spirituality and experiential conversion and second, its anti-body nature. To support the possible Gnosticism suggested by these two characteristics, we'll reflect on the movement's revivalist roots going back to the influence of Gnosticism upon second and third-century Christianity, Protestantism, Pietism and the two American Great Awakenings. All of which is to say, Evangelicalism's vulnerability and similarity to Gnosticism are both historical and theological.

Inner Spirituality and Experiential Conversion

Before the end of the first century, the Apostle John discovered the first lie of culture perpetrated on the church. It was Gnosticism, a Greek-based ideology characterized by belief in both the evil of Creation and the human body. The body was evil; only the spirit was good. Salvation was earned by having elite knowledge leading to the experience of escaping the body. John's last letters addressed the inner spirituality of Gnostics as counter to the church. He created a test for any spirituality confronting the nascent community of believers: only a spirituality which affirmed that Jesus Christ came in a fleshly body represented Christianity. All mystical experiences, however exciting and dramatic, which didn't lead to belief that the Word who became flesh were false and to be rejected as non-Christian.

To summarize, a Gnostic must demonstrate an inner experience rooted in one's internal divinity which progressed spiritually through special knowledge. No spiritual connection existed forming a community of Gnostics requiring that they care for one another. It was all about the self. We now compare Gnosticism with Evangelicalism.

Evangelicalism does not exist without the inner experience of being born again. An Evangelical is separated out from any other Christian who has not had such an experience. That is, Evangelicals possess a special knowledge. An Evangelical is a special type of Christian. Evangelicals often appear to display a spiritual superiority over non-born-again Christians. It is only recently that Evangelicals have rejected their narrow-mindedness to risk saying that Catholics may be Christians. Ironically, Roman Catholics possess a more biblical concept of the church than self-centered Evangelicals who have left the church. That is, Evangelicals have often been spiritually proud of the fact that their lack of participation in the church is less important to their conversion than an elusive mystical experience which may or may not include the Holy Spirit. To be clear, one's decision to be born again doesn't save anyone. Rather the Apostle Paul speaks of being saved by what God has done. Grace through faith versus works permeates Paul's letters to churches. A decision is what a person does. Grace is what God does. It is far better to know who Jesus Christ is today than to camp on a decision made years ago with no evidence that Jesus is Lord of one's life now.

Conversion by experience is meaningless outside the church where the Word is proclaimed, the Holy Spirit is present, the sacraments are practiced decently and in order, confession and forgiveness are in evidence and the cross is central. A church might be dead according to some individual arbitrary standard, but it is still the church. That community might be sinful and in need of repentance just as the Corinthian church was. The Apostle constantly challenged the churches he planted to repent continually. But he never told even the most sinful community of Christians that they were no longer a church. When sin was discovered and admitted, Paul instructed that those who were spiritual were to restore the sinner. Knowing that Gnostic thought lurked behind the corner, the Apostle John warned, "If we say that we have no sin, we deceive ourselves and the truth is not in us." An inability to admit sin is tantamount to Gnosticism's rejection of sin's existence. Any form of self-righteous Evangelicalism is Gnostic. Self-deception doesn't disband a church. Confession is always possible. Forgiveness is always available. God's grace and mercy are central to the gospel. Gnosticism has no concept of grace or mercy. Without sin, you don't need either. The only problem is to think that no sin exists is detached from reality. If we're to take sin seriously, and God did, we need to exchange self-righteousness for humility.

To the degree that Evangelicalism continues to insist on the practice of an inner spiritual experience of conversion, an experience which is unverifiable, it is at least vulnerable to Gnosticism or at worst, Gnostic. An exclusive decision-based spirituality is foreign to the gospel. The grace of God through faith involves a process of being saved which may include a definite decision. But the Apostle Paul urges the church to "work out its salvation with fear and trembling."[1] That is, being saved is a process involving one's body, mind, soul, and spirit. Gnosticism would never speak of working out one's salvation; especially a salvation which includes the body. To the degree that Evangelicalism has used language for salvation which excludes the body, it has been Gnostic. Having identified the possibility of Gnosticism within Evangelicalism, we now briefly review other historic *isms* from which Evangelicalism is derived. Such movements also derive in part from Gnosticism. To the degree that Evangelicalism is a para-church movement, it has followed in Pietism's footsteps.

1. Philippians 2: 13

Evangelicalism Is Dead

Evangelicalism emanates from a Pietistic-revivalism which spawned the Cane Ridge camp meeting and two Great Awakenings. Recall the bizarre experiences converted souls had at Cane Ridge. "Many fell down, as men slain battle . . . breathless and motionless . . . a deep groan . . . a piercing shriek . . . a prayer for mercy."[2] Here was the *doctrine of experience*. Harold Bloom was a self-professed Gnostic, not a Christian by any imagined stretch. Yet, he's the one who sees Evangelicalism for what it is. Experience replaced Calvinism *as doctrine*. This is precisely the point. By abandoning the church, it also neglected the foundational doctrines of the Scripture. The Incarnation was neglected in the name of spirituality. No one at Cane Ridge had a head jerk followed by a statement affirming that Jesus came in the flesh. The Great Awakenings became the church in a forest with little impact on the well-being of a local congregation of card-carrying Presbyterians, Methodists or Baptists with ordained pastors. Peter Burfeind described the individualized spiritualism as "Salvation for the American, cannot come through the congregation, but in a one to one act of confrontation . . . a total inward solitude. Doctrinally, we may arguably state that Evangelicalism portrays salvation through such experiences which may lead to abstracting Christ from his humanity which cuts out the heart of the Incarnation."

To summarize this section about inner spirituality and experiential conversion, every movement prior to the naming of Evangelicalism emphasized some type of unverifiable inner spiritual experience. To be fair, the emotional events that occurred at Cane Ridge didn't happen, for example, at the 1957 New York Billy Graham crusade both of which endeavored to save souls. The spiritual experiences at Cane Ridge or any future revival may have included an authentic movement of the Holy Spirit in a person's life. But Evangelicalism's insistence upon an experienced-based salvation to the minimization of intellectual belief and behavioral repentance fell prey to Gnosticism. If Scripture is your rule for faith and practice, you cannot standardize one's inner feeling of conversion to Christ. Evangelicalism's major flaw is that while stating the key

---

2. Bloom, *American Religion*, 60.

role of Scripture and preaching its content, its hidden agenda is really internal spirituality. Harold Bloom may have best summed up the issue this way—"The evangelical needs neither theology nor liturgy . . . no intellectual pursuit nor tradition . . . you can float in safety on the little raft of your inward piety."

Anti-Body

Just as Gnostic thought has invaded Evangelicalism evidenced by standardizing on inward piety and experiential conversion for salvation, it also demotes and denigrates the body. Evangelicalism has historically lacked a theology of the body. It comes by this honestly, for it sought only to save souls. The body was considered outside the parameters of redemption. Only the spirit was involved in salvation. The human body and its behaviors were spoken about only within the context of morality, or more accurately, immorality. Pope John Paul II offered the church the most comprehensively theological analysis of the body. This Pope did battle with Gnosticism. In his *Man and Woman Created He Them: A Theology of the Body*, he said that "A theology of the body should not astonish or surprise anyone who is aware of the mystery and reality of the Incarnation. Through the fact that the Word of God became flesh, the body entered theology through the main door." Here we have a theological basis for the sanctity of the human body as a sign of the person and how it reveals the nature of God. Like Gnosticism, Evangelicalism found that the body was unworthy of salvation and violated an integration of body, mind, soul, and spirit within all persons.

Sadly, Evangelicalism is completely empty regarding any theology of the body. Since spiritual experience is the movie's title, a theology of the body has ended up on the cutting room floor. A theology of the body derives from the very creation of the first man and woman both of whom were created from matter. Adam from dirt and Eve from a human rib. Though created from matter both were made in the image of God. To the extent that Evangelicalism has stressed spirit to the neglect of the body, it has fallen prey to a denigration of the body. To be fair, there is no reason to believe that Evangelicals did this intentionally. Because theology was minimized, the movement may have had little idea how close it came to Gnosticism.

The Apostle's Creed addresses Gnosticism in its opening statement about God, as Creator of heaven and earth—spiritual and physical. God called all the visible items of creation good from trees to insects. Also, note the last statement in the Creed: "the resurrection of the body." This is based upon the bodily resurrection of Jesus Christ. Valuing the body is what distinguished Christianity from all other religions of the time. Immorality of the soul came from Greek thought. The sanctity of the body and its resurrection were original with Christianity. The early church proclaimed a God who became human.

Evangelicalism's anti-body stance derives from its rejection of the church, the body of Christ. It would have been inconsistent for Evangelicalism to leave the body of Christ and then formulate a theology of the body. The implications are severe. In Gnosticism, the body as evil can only do evil. So the body doesn't deserve to be saved. There should be no surprise then that the body continually behaves sinfully. Because that's all it can do. What else can you expect? This Gnostic attitude is prevalent in any argument by a Christian scholar, pastor or church leader leaving sexual behavior an open question as far as Christianity is concerned, especially within the current debate on same-sex marriage. If the body is inherently evil, all sexual behavior is non-redeemable and destined to be evil itself. The cross, it is thought, covers only the spiritual, not the physical according to misinformed Evangelicals. Same-sex marriage flies in the face of the definition of marriage between one man and one woman who cleave to one another and become one flesh. Same-sex marriage is an oxymoron. Same-sex marriage perverts the most sacred analogy from the Apostle Paul who relates Christ's relationship to the church as that of husband to wife. In *Against the Protestant Gnostics*, Peter Burfeind speaks of a holistic gospel pertaining to both spirit and body: "The revelation of Christ pertains to matters of both the spirit and the kingdom of the flesh." Christianity, the true alternative to Gnosticism's false view of the body, finds all persons redeemable as an integration of mind-body-soul-spirit. Because Jesus Christ bore our sins in his body on the cross, God was saying that the human body created in our image is worthy of redemption.

Evangelicalism's disdain for sacraments emanates from a Gnostic notion that the ordinary cannot be sacred or spiritual. Jesus said, "This is my body" when holding up a loaf of bread. That loaf of bread was matter; it was sacramental as an ordinary part of creation made holy as representing Christ's own body mysteriously comprised of flesh and spirit. Jesus was not one person with an evil nature and a good nature. Jesus was one person with two natures—divine and human, both of which were good. Any diminishing of the sacraments of the church is on the slippery slope toward Gnosticism. That the divine appeared human without looking divine is the essence of the Incarnation. Had the Word become spirit, who would have recognized him? Had God become mind, who would have known him? Jesus was a mystery, but at least you could see, hear and touch him. This is why the Apostle John's first letter begins with "We declare to you what we have heard . . . seen . . . looked at . . . and touched." Thomas touched the wounds of Jesus and believed. The physical body of Jesus is the basis for his statement at the Last Supper. It is the manger showing up at the table of the Lord. The tangible sacrificial lamb of the Jewish Passover which was always *on the table* is now the sacrificial lamb *at the table* showing us bread as his body and wine as his blood. This transfer from *on the table* to *at the table* is the new covenant Jesus mentioned at that last meal with his followers. Jesus is the Lamb of God who takes away the sin of the world. He is the host. Jesus is the original sacrament. Christians are reminded that they become "little sacraments" after they have tasted and seen that the Lord is good in the Eucharist.

A clear application of anti-body Evangelicalism characterized its defense of slavery in the first two decades of the nineteenth century in the South. Southern Evangelicals were active on behalf of women's rights and prison reform. However, when advocating human rights meant confronting the evils of slavery, southern Evangelicals adopted what they called "the spirituality of the Church."[3] This doctrine held that the Church was permitted no official involvement in the social reform of the state. This teaching was prompted by the South's need to distinguish itself from the North by withdrawing into separate Christian communities. The South was the sacred community; the North was the world. This is blatant racism couched in religious jargon. The Gnosticism behind such denial of the humanity of African Americans is obvious. This opposition to Jesus-come-in-the-flesh failed the Apostle John's test for authentic spirituality. The doctrine of the "spirituality of the church" continues in various forms to this day. While southern Evangelicals arbitrarily absented themselves from mere issues of justice, such indeed as issues of racial justice. The racism inherent in southern Evangelicalism had roots in the earlier revivals. "Neither George Whitefield nor the American revival preachers raised direct questions about the institution of slavery."[4] The Civil Rights movement of the 1960's was dominated by theological liberalism's reduction of the gospel to human needs devoid of the cross. Only after Civil Rights legislation was enacted did Evangelicals slowly become involved in social justice issues. Today, Evangelicalism has voiced its confused positions regarding the gay issue. However, without a theology of the body, some Evangelicals continue to reject Scriptural statements about behavior for both heterosexuals and homosexuals. Further, without a theology of the body, Evangelicalism often falls prey to the mistaken notion that matters of body are non-essential to the gospel. This ignorance of a holistic gospel represents Evangelicalism's reduction of the Good News to issues of spirituality at the expense of the human body. This is a denial of the Incarnation and a rejection of Jesus' mandate of liberation in Luke 4 and his statements which identify himself as the poor, homeless, lonely and imprisoned in Matthew 25. Sadly, to this day, so-called Evangelical churches are far too Caucasian and struggle to include of all races, tribes, tongues and nations.

3. Fitzgerald, *The Evangelicals*, 53.
4. Ahlstrom, 657–69.

That is, despite all rhetoric to the contrary, racism within Evangelicalism persists as evidenced by an NAE (National Association of Evangelicals) which didn't include African Americans requiring what blacks have always needed to do—start their own separate organization, the National Black Evangelical Association.

This chapter has attempted to show that Evangelicalism is at best vulnerable to Gnosticism and at worst a form of Gnosticism itself. A review of Evangelicalism's roots in Protestantism, Pietism and revivalism reveals an inner spirituality and experiential conversion combined with a rejection of the body. For Evangelicalism, Gnosticism has been the sin that leads to death.

We now turn our attention to Fundamentalism, yet another emanation of Evangelicalism which reacted militantly against late nineteenth-century and early twentieth-century modernism and theological liberalism.

Chapter 9

Fundamentalism

NOW THAT WE HAVE a working definition of Evangelicalism and have demonstrated its vulnerability to Gnosticism, we're ready to get into movements which have influenced Evangelicalism beginning with Fundamentalism. At this point we begin to see Evangelicalism's relationship to culture in the following ways: withdrawal, engagement, transformation, accommodation and absorption. Fundamentalism *withdrew* from culture to create its own separatist subculture. Rather than use reason to combat modernism and theological liberalism, it simply used the Bible as a hammer to make its case.

Fundamentalism is defined as a strict adherence to a core set of principles. *Fundamentalism* was coined as a term in 1920 as a reaction against a so-called higher critical way to interpret Scripture which preferred the historical, cultural and social background of biblical texts to grammatical analysis of a biblical passage. Fundamentalism took on a combative opposition to modernity and science. Liberalism explained away all of Jesus' miracles, the possibility of bodily resurrection, and avoided any mention of a visible and bodily re-appearance of Jesus Christ. It should be noted that founding-father Thomas Jefferson rewrote the New Testament by literally cutting out the miracles in the Gospels. A more recent example of Bible-tampering surfaced in the *Jesus Seminar* where scholars color-coded those statements which Jesus would have never said, those which he might have said and those he did say. This figurative scissoring of the Gospels applied higher critical interpretation to biblical texts with crayons. Its faddism has come and gone and is no longer taken seriously.

The Fundamentals,[1] twelve booklets, explicitly reduced Christianity to five core principles all of which were directed at modernism and theological liberalism. We name them here for analysis later. They are the inerrancy of the Bible, the reality of miracles, the virgin birth, the bodily resurrection of Jesus Christ, and the substitutionary atonement of Christ on the cross. Fundamentalism is a vast topic which goes into more names, events and details beyond the scope of this book. It was the first external movement to reduce classic Evangelicalism to a list of five important doctrines.

Fundamentalism's reaction to culture was withdrawal as a separatist phenomenon creating its own sub-culture. As a trans-denominational movement, it had no home in a particular local congregation and maintained Evangelicalism's historic opposition to the church. While certain local bodies may have been described as fundamentalist churches, the word rarely, if at all, appeared on a church marquis. New Bible churches and Bible colleges emerged reflecting their agreement with the five fundamentals. We now focus on those five particular principles which defined Fundamentalism as a reduction of the Christian faith and church. In each case we will show that Fundamentalism could have met science and theological liberalism on their own turf. It would make no sense to merely quote verses from the Bible as proof to those who didn't accept the Bible as valid. As a result, this reductionist movement of Christianity proceeded to intellectually demean the Scripture in particular and Christianity in general.

---

1. Marsden, *Fundamentalism and American Culture*, 118.

Inerrancy of Scripture

Inerrancy means (lit., "free from error") and is aligned with *infallible* (when applied to religion, "incapable of error when defining doctrines"). *Inerrancy* aligns with *infallible* over the issue of *doctrine, not specific words, phrases or clauses*. The battle for the Bible according to Harold Lindsell, the poster child for inerrancy, led the charge. Inerrancy was about the letter of the law, not its spirit. There was little born-again spirituality during this heated dialogue among Evangelicals and Fundamentalists. In *Fundamentalism and American Culture*, George Marsden states that Evangelicalism never achieved a "working hypothesis for most Evangelicals to interact with the humanity of Scripture in general and biblical criticism in particular." This means that only spiritual matters were important. By now, you recognize this as Gnosticism. That said, Fundamentalism offered no intellectual way to live creatively with theology and biblical criticism. It claimed more for Scripture than Scripture claimed for itself. This was only one symptom of Fundamentalism's anti-intellectualism.

In some corners of Fundamentalism, inerrancy became a litmus test for faith. That is, not only did one need the born again experience, but also needed a letter-perfect view of the Bible. Evangelicals seemed to claim a common biblical norm yet taught contradictory theology. Suffice it say, inerrancy bore little fruit within the Fundamentalist-Evangelical camp where it was obvious that they were known more by their stubbornness than by their love. Having addressed the debacle of inerrancy, something the Bible never claimed for itself, we now turn our attention to a second core principle: the reality of the supernatural, or miracles.

Miracles

The second core principle of Fundamentalism was the reality of supernatural events, otherwise known as miracles recorded in the Bible. Liberalism's narrow-minded challenge to miracles was a function of a rationalism emanating from nineteenth century

Germany. It was the dominance of science primarily evident in Darwinism. We've already observed how higher criticism challenged a historical-grammatical interpretation of the Bible. To read the actual words of Scripture literally according to their dictionary meanings, succumbed to paying more attention to the space in between the lines related to social location, culture and an author's personality when interpreting a text. So the meaningless discussion of the actual length of a day became more important than whether Jesus was God or not.

The scientific method cannot apply to proving or disproving miracles. For example, the notion of determining a hypothesis, designing an experiment to support the supposition followed by data collection which may be analyzed to support or falsify the fact that God created the world is absurd. The scientific method is limited to proving *only repeatable events* which may be reconstructed in a laboratory for experimentation. Creation would be quite difficult to reproduce in a science lab. Imagine applying the scientific method to verify a virgin birth, a bodily resurrection or a man walking on water! The scientific method is useless to determine the truth of one-time non-repeatable events. Fundamentalists failed to see the weakness of science and chose to unreasonably proof-text their way through all the challenges brought up against Christianity.

Ironically, the best that Fundamentalism could do to challenge liberal anti-supernaturalism was to employ an aspect of the mind neglected in its own definition—reason. Recall that the four points which define Evangelicalism are conversion, the Bible, the Cross and mission. Reason is absent; yet used by some Fundamentalists to argue their case for miracles. Warfield, a Princeton Seminary theologian, was a champion of the rational or reasonable defense of Christianity. Later, Evangelicals would get into apologetics, the defense of the faith, as a rational approach to state their case. Along with inerrancy and miracles, another major principle of Fundamentalism was the virgin birth.

Virgin Birth

Christianity has historically used *virgin birth* as the operative phrase to speak of the supernatural uniqueness of the birth of Jesus of Nazareth, the Son of God. Yet, a brief review of the text where Gabriel announces to Mary her role to give birth to the savior of the world indicates that the miracle involves God, not Mary. A natural birth without male-female intercourse is impossible. The overshadowing of Mary by the Holy Spirit is supernatural. The process is the unnatural birth; the agent is the Holy Spirit. If Fundamentalism wanted to identify Jesus' birth as miraculous, the core principle should have been the *overshadowing of the Holy Spirit*. That's the supernatural aspect of the virgin birth. The role of the Holy Spirit is the real issue, not what happened to Mary. The *who* involved in the so-called virgin birth is more important than the *how*. Agency overrides process.

The Apostle John sees this issue when he refers to the hovering of the Holy Spirit over the Tabernacle from the history of Israel. In John 1: 14, he says, "The Word became flesh and *dwelt among us* . . . " Literally, *dwelt among us* may be translated as *tabernacled among us*. The Tabernacle is the temporary house of worship for the Hebrew people through the desert after leaving Egypt. As a verb, *tabernacle* can mean "to inhabit a physical body." This is how we need to understand what's happening to Mary. So the Incarnation, God arriving on earth as a human baby, is the presence of God as the glorious mist hovering over the temporary sanctuary of Israel. This supernatural phenomenon anticipates the Holy Spirit's hovering over Jesus at his baptism, the filling of the disciples on resurrection night and Pentecost.

Physiologically, there is no scientific proof of the overshadowing of a human being by a spirit. This is a one-time occurrence. Therefore, the virgin birth of Jesus Christ is neither proven nor disproven by the scientific method since it applies only to repeatable events. Fundamentalism was right to state that the virgin birth was a miracle. But it didn't get into the historical, linguistic and theological background of Christ's birth. This omission evidences

Fundamentalism's anti-intellectualism. Bonhoeffer sums up the theological value of the virgin birth by focusing on the question, "Who is this baby?" rather than bogging down on the question, "How did this baby get here?" He employs a both-and approach here which typically resolves the apparent contradictions within theology. He adheres to the biblical witness in its claim for the uniqueness of how Mary conceived of her baby while at the same time focusing on the uniqueness of who her baby was as the Son of God. Clearly, it's more important for a Christian to have a personal relationship with Mary's son than to be able to explain how he arrived on earth. Given this focus on the body related to the Incarnation, we now focus upon the next core principle—the bodily resurrection of Jesus Christ.

Bodily Resurrection

The historical possibility of supernatural events, miracles, continues as a core principle of Fundamentalism when it lists Jesus' bodily rising from the dead. Now that we realize the deficiency of science to prove or disprove miracles, we need to ask ourselves this question. Are the documents which state the resurrection reliable? Are the Gospel authors who claim to have seen the reappearance of Jesus credible witnesses? If so, then we have a basis for belief in what they claim to have seen. The Gospels are reliable, that is infallible, based upon the consistency of eyewitness accounts from five hundred people, primarily the same persons who knew Jesus over three years and recognized him after his death. Either the biblical claim of resurrection is false or true. The issue is not so much about the Bible as it is about the possibility of supernatural events themselves. Modernism's hang up is its inadequate view of reality, not the false news of a resurrection concocted by Jesus' disciples to verify their faith. Mary's ultimate response to Gabriel about her role in giving birth to the Son of the Most High applies here: "All things are possible with God." Not to believe in a God who is beyond the verifiability of science, it to believe in no God at all. Essentially, the basis for belief in the virgin birth and the resurrection is the same. The authenticity of Scripture and its claims override any ability of science to disprove those claims. We now focus on the important teaching of the cross as it relates to a person's salvation—the substitutionary atonement.

Substitutionary Atonement

Finally, the fifth core principle of Fundamentalism lists the substitutionary atonement of Jesus on the cross for sin, sins and sinners. That is, Jesus Christ died on a cross instead of us sinners. Jesus often spoke of his suffering and death. Recall how Peter objected and wanted to be protective. Jesus' last mention of this occurs at the Last Supper where he speaks of the new covenant in his blood previously announced by the prophet Jeremiah centuries before Jesus arrived on earth. This prophetic text is quoted by the author of Hebrews speaking of Jesus as superior to Moses as a priest. Recalling our earlier discussion of the Gospel, we simply reference Bonhoeffer's discussion of atonement added to substitutionary atonement. While Fundamentalism had it right to challenge liberalism of Christ's cross theological meaning for salvation, it failed to mention that Jesus Christ not only took our place on the cross, but also became our ongoing advocate. That is, Jesus died *instead of us* and *for us*. The biblical robust gospel combines both elements of a substitutionary and vicarious atonement.

To summarize, the objective of this chapter has been to define and analyze one of Evangelicalism's emanations: Fundamentalism. We've noted its militant attitude toward both a scientifically informed modernism and theological liberalism. Fundamentalism was an anti-intellectual reaction against science, historical criticism of Scripture and the denial of the supernatural aspects of Christianity. It unwittingly reduced the credibility of Scripture by misusing it as a hammer when it could have used reasonable argument to challenge modernism and theological liberalism. What it didn't say and its negative tone destroyed its credibility. Carl Henry's prophecy in 1947 about Fundamentalism has come to pass. " . . . Fundamentalism in two generations will be reduced to a . . . despised and oppressive sect."[2] It may even be worse than Henry's prediction. Today, *Fundamentalism* is virtually absent as a religious concept. Its response to culture by *withdrawal* and separatism has wiped out the term from current Christian vocabulary. Carl Henry, along with others, saw this coming and urged a new type of Evangelicalism. We now get into Neo-Evangelicalism whose objective would be a scholarly *engagement* with culture.

---

2. Henry, *The Uneasy Conscience of Modern Fundamentalism*, xv.

Chapter 10

New Evangelicalism

IN THIS CHAPTER we take a look at Neo-Evangelicalism, or New Evangelicalism. It was new compared to classic Evangelicalism discussed earlier. It was a post-WWII reaction against the anti-intellectualism of Fundamentalism. It rejected withdrawal from culture by trying to *engage* culture. It was time for a more scholarly approach which involved the creation of new publications (*Christianity Today*), new seminaries (*Fuller*) and the advent of Billy Graham's mass evangelism. It would differ from Fundamentalism's separatism and enter into dialogue with liberals rather than hurl rocks at them. Neo-Evangelicalism was characterized by a mood of positivism and non-militancy. These new Evangelicals would meet humanists on their own turf. Neo-Evangelicalism created the space for Evangelicalism's attachment to politics in the form of ethics and morality.

True to its historic form, Evangelicalism has never had a central governing authority.[1] Informed by its early anti-church tradition, it has consistently favored an individualism which works against an overarching home office. However, Neo-Evangelicalism ushered in a "pope" in Billy Graham who joined Jonathan Edwards, George Whitefield and D.L. Moody as a prominent name within the movement. The National Association of Evangelicals

---

1. Worthen, *Apostles of Reason*, 36–55.

New Evangelicalism

was founded by Harold Ockenga, co-founder of Fuller Seminary, as a voluntary association of evangelical churches with the following shared creed written in 2012:

> We believe the Bible to be the inspired, the only infallible, authoritative Word of God. We believe that there is one God, eternally existent in three persons: Father, Son and Holy Spirit. We believe in the deity of the Lord Jesus Christ, in His virgin birth, in His sinless life, in His miracles, in His vicarious and atoning death through His shed blood, in His bodily resurrection, in His ascension to the right hand of the Father, and in His personal return in power and glory. We believe that for salvation of lost and sinful people, regeneration by the Holy Spirit is absolutely essential. We believe in the present ministry of the Holy Spirit by whose indwelling the Christian is enabled to live a godly life. We believe in the resurrection of both the saved and the lost; they that are saved unto the resurrection of life and they that are lost unto the resurrection of damnation. We believe in the spiritual unity of believers in Jesus Christ.

This Evangelical creed merits comment at several of its points. First, note the absence of *inerrancy* in the statement about the Word of God. *Inspired* is used as the only word Scripture ever claims for itself; *infallible* is essentially synonymous with inerrant without drawing attention to past controversy; *authoritative* is notable by its explicit mention, though implicit in the origin of Evangelicalism. Second, note the absence of *substitutionary* for the atonement and the presence of *vicarious*. This is a theological step forward for Evangelicalism. As stated before, Christ not only takes our place on the cross but continues to intercede for us as our ongoing advocate before the Father. Third, its statement about salvation is a theological improvement over Evangelicalism's historic emphasis on the born-again experience favoring God's agency with regeneration by the Holy Spirit. Fourth, the use of *present* to describe the ministry of the Holy Spirit represents a challenge to fundamentalism's insistence that the activity of the Holy Spirit's ceased with the end of the first century. This no doubt represents the participation of

Pentecostals in Evangelicalism from their inception with the early twentieth century Azusa Street Revival. Sixth, resurrection of all human beings the Apostles' Creed. In fact, this Evangelical Creed simply repeats the theology of that historic creed. Evangelicalism consistently separated itself from the church by maintaining that it needed no creed but the Bible. Not before the twenty-first century did Evangelicalism document its creed and attempt to link up with the last two thousand years of church history.

Finally and most importantly, *spiritual unity of believers* is a far cry from "we believe one holy catholic and apostolic church" from the Apostle's Creed. True to its anti-church origins, the NAE couldn't bring itself to say *church*. Anti-clericalism and anti-tradition have historically dominated the scene within Evangelicalism. We've already noted that *evangelical church* is really an oxymoron since church is never mentioned in any definition of Evangelicalism. Evangelicalism has always been para-church, *never within the church*. Evangelicalism's intent to fix the church has no support from the New Testament where Paul always worked within the church to deal with heresy and errant behavior. As we've stated, Evangelicalism's largest flaw has been its inability to state a theology of the church. This is why Evangelicalism gravitated to culture. Having reviewed NAE's Creed of Evangelicalism, we now briefly look into Fuller Seminary's Statement of Faith, *What We Evangelicals Believe*. Taken together, both statements characterize an attempt to make Evangelicalism more credible as a scholarly movement engaged with culture.

Fuller Seminary's creed had the following categories: historic Christianity, Neo-Evangelicalism, globalism, ecumenism, and the kingdom of God. First, charting the history of the church was positioned as a lens through which Scripture must be read. This challenged Evangelicalism's historic anti-church and anti-tradition stance. It was a breakthrough by reexamining the early church fathers and the early creeds. Implied here was the encouragement to engage in social concerns as Christians, to be involved politically and to resurface from subcultural Fundamentalism. Second, a new Christian identity which was neither Fundamentalism nor liberalism was formed. Instead of separating themselves from doctrinally impure churches or from secular culture itself, Neo-Evangelicalism sought to address the social and political issues of the day. It initiated dialogue with the Jewish community from which Christianity is derived. Fuller also broadened itself by intentionally admitting students from other cultures. A breakthrough in Evangelical seminary education was achieved by Fuller's embracing of the charismatic community. Third, Fuller's intention to see itself globally included its multiethnic, international and interracial make-up. Global Christianity was further enhanced by the use of communication technology to advance the gospel message. Fourth, ecumenism within Christian movements and denominations characterized Neo-Evangelicalism. Beyond historic Evangelical mission agencies either denominational or independent, Neo-Evangelicalism encouraged participation in Christian social action projects such as Bread for the World and Habitat for Humanity. Fuller was on the cutting edge of what would become a deeper involvement by Evangelicals in issues of justice, compassion and mercy. The attempt was to balance saving bodiless souls along with ministry to the needs of bodily needs of real human beings. This may be viewed as doing battle with Gnosticism, even though Evangelicals never stated themselves as combatants of this historic heresy of the church. Finally, this statement of faith included the unique category of *The Movement of the Reign of God*. This was new language for Evangelicals. Here was an emphasis to move the church beyond its walls to encounter the working of God through the Holy Spirit for peace and justice in the world. Recall that Jesus, without marginalizing the church as Evangelicalism had done, stressed the kingdom of God.

While Fuller Seminary offered a refreshing change as a poster child for Neo-Evangelicalism, there was at least one downside. Engagement with culture carried with it an inability to be countercultural when needed. Engagement often traded off biblical principle in the name of not being too Fundamentalistic. Biblical models of mission were challenged by church growth theories spawned in the 1970s by Donald McGavran and Peter Wagner. Essentially, their notion of growing a Christian congregation was anti-biblical. It traded off diversity for uniformity. They called it the *Homogeneous Unit Principle* for church growth. It was based upon the need to make outsiders more comfortable. It plain language it was based upon the biblically-challenged principle birds of a feather flock together. One way to grow a church would be along similar ethnic lines: white churches, black churches, or Spanish-speaking churches. The strategy was tribal. It rejected Pentecost. It failed. It was a clear example of scholarly replacement of Scripture with an imported church growth theory from tribes in India which didn't work in the United States. People in America don't convert in tribes. McGavran and Wagner misread the tea leaves regarding the cultural individualism of Americans. Years later they recanted their failed attempt to grow the American church using methods from other cultures. Both failed to notice that along with other nations, America, too, had its own cultural norms within which the gospel could be contextualized.

Of course, the name most associated with Neo-Evangelicalism has to be the world renowned evangelist Billy Graham. Heralded as one of the most influential Christian leaders of the twentieth century, Graham resurrected the Great Awakenings now conducted in athletic stadiums around the world. His unfortunately named crusades involved both mainline and evangelical churches. His name is virtually attached to all innovations brought into existence with Neo-Evangelicalism. Billy Graham preached the gospel to more people in person than anyone in the history of Christianity. Grant Wacker said this about him: "His presence conferred status on presidents, acceptability of wars, shame on racial prejudice, desirability on decency, dishonor on indecency, and prestige on civic events." Graham's iconic photo of circus tents in Los Angeles depicted his mass evangelism, the dominant activity of his varied ministry. His London crusade lasted 3 months; the New York crusade in 1957 went on for 4 months. His crusades began segregated, but in 1953 he tore down the ropes during a rally in Chattanooga. He had a close relationship with Martin Luther King, Jr., but had to recant the anti-Semitic comment he made

New Evangelicalism

recorded in a conversation with Nixon. He was invited to speak at the 9/11 memorial service at the National Cathedral on September 14, 2001. Billy Graham died in 2018 and lay in state at the Capitol Rotunda, only the fourth private citizen so honored. Graham is no doubt the only Evangelical graced with a star on the famous sidewalk in Hollywood.

No discussion of Neo-Evangelicalism would be complete without mentioning Carl F. H. Henry. He wanted an intellectually and culturally engaged Evangelicalism and a worldview based solidly on biblical authority. Henry urged Evangelicalism to experience a rebirth of apostolic passion to head off becoming either a cult or a despised sect; new language for a tradition-denying movement. Paul's "Damascus Road" experience caused him to repent of murdering Christians and catapulted him into planting churches around the world. Thomas' rebirth had him take the gospel to southern India where *Mar Thoma* churches exist today. Henry's was a call to being born from above which urged Christians to repent, follow Jesus as Lord and take leaps of action for God. Neo-Evangelicalism called for a Christian world view which embraced societal needs which rises from the Great Commission as much as evangelism does. A new possibility of balancing ministry to both body and spirit appeared possible captured in Jesus' statement to the paralyzed man let down through the roof "Which is easier to say 'your sins are forgiven,' or to say 'Stand up and walk' ... ?" Here we find clear biblical evidence for a holistic gospel fleshing out of Jesus' manifesto to "preach good news to the poor, release to captives, sight to the blind and liberty to the oppressed ... "

George Marsden actually thought that the 1960s held the possibility for an Evangelical alliance which might coordinate evangelism, education, publication and social action. However, just over a decade later he realized his dream had failed. Key to the failure was replacing the church with an alliance. Again we see a movement outside the church driven by an idea foreign to the New Testament. For what characterized Neo-Evangelicalism more than anything was its propensity to create coalitions, organizations, campus ministries and other parachurch emanations. Carl Henry continued to see the possibility of remaking the modern mind. Mark Noll would later write *The Scandal of the Evangelical Mind* (1994). Sadly, the sought-after intellectualism failed to replace the mindlessness of Fundamentalism. It seemed that Neo-Evangelicalism's engagement with culture had no other home than politics. Its failed attempt to transform culture resulted in a newly-discovered attachment to conservative politics represented by Republican Party platforms one of whose planks was moral reform of society.

Beyond identifying with the forty-odd denominations of the NAE, Neo-Evangelicalism would now be defined by other movements like Falwell's Moral Majority. The aftermath of Watergate created space for improved ethical behavior among government officials starting with the president. What better president than a Southern Baptist Sunday school teacher named Jimmy Carter? He would usher in the *Year of the Evangelical* announced by *Newsweek* in 1976. Evangelicalism came of age. Religion and politics would mix in America. The Reagan years of the 1980s appeared to align the Oval Office with the pulpit. A new Religious Right would emerge which echoed Fundamentalism. As many as fifty million Americans identified as Evangelical responding to a Gallup poll.

A specific alliance with both ethical and political features would be Neo-Evangelicalism's outspoken voice against abortion in America. Here we have unmistakable definition on an issue. The Pro-Life movement in the United States, initiated by the Roman Catholic church and empowered by the Moral Majority, challenged the Pro-Choice movement which heralded a woman's right to the use of her body to terminate a pregnancy without discussion of the choice she made to become pregnant. Pro-Choice was a half-truth. The abortion question dominated how Evangelicals exercised their concern for social justice by giving voice to a voiceless human being. Political debates raged in Congress. Politicians now knew when life actually began within the womb! Evangelicals quoted Psalm 139 to speak of how God actually knew a pre-born infant as He intervened in human life from conception throughout early development. Evangelicals stood outside abortion clinics with Catholic nuns protesting the murder of human beings. Along with the moral and ethical challenges related to abortion, a political resistance to court-based legislation occurred. Contrary to the Constitution, the Supreme Court stepped outside its jurisdiction and made a law literally overnight with no input from the United States Congress.

To recap this chapter we've identified Neo-Evangelicalism as a reaction against Fundamentalism. It sought to engage culture rather than to withdraw from it. It included America's mass evangelist Billy Graham who along with Carl Henry sought an intellectualism and scholarship to compete with theological liberals. We saw how it failed to do so and to this day remains hidden in its own subculture less militant than Fundamentalism. Evangelicalism has historically defined itself by alliances and the evolution of movements we've compared to Gnostic emanations. Typical of Evangelicalism's reactionary DNA, two new opposing Evangelical movements surfaced—Contemporary and Emergent Christianity—both of which, unfortunately, modeled effective ways to accommodate culture into the church. In the next chapter we see how these two movements incorporated consumerism into the church so that its customers were satisfied with its brand.

Chapter 11

Contemporary and Emergent Evangelicalism

IN THE LAST CHAPTER WE DISCUSSED Neo-Evangelicalism as a reaction against Fundamentalism. In this chapter we take a look at the evolution of Evangelicalism into a pair of opposing submovements. First, we'll look into Contemporary Evangelicalism as a shift in liturgy and church structure. Second, we'll get into how the short-lived Emergent Church evolved as a reaction against Contemporary Evangelicalism. Both movements represented unique ways to *accommodate* culture into the church. While various forms of Contemporary Evangelicalism still exist, the Emergent Church has been taken off the table as a viable movement within Evangelicalism.

Contemporary Evangelicalism

This phenomenon alters Christian worship to meet the consumer needs of a disgruntled or unchurched audience. At all costs to the integrity of historic Christian liturgy, relevance is the authority. The target audience for this counterfeit of Christian worship are named seekers. That is, seekers of God who are turned off by the organized church. Compare this to Jesus' words where *he* claimed to be the seeker of the lost from Luke's Gospel. Consider also the

Contemporary and Emergent Evangelicalism

Garden of Eden where *God* seeks Adam and Eve. It was clear that they weren't seeking him. The objective of this chapter is to expose the non-biblical basis for not only a so-called contemporary style in worship designed more for "seekers" than for God, but also a worship before the altar of relevance and consumerism.

Along with its historic disdain for the church, this brand of Evangelicalism fell prey to celebrity-ism accompanied by a lack of accountability among church leaders. Truth be told, it appeared that catering to human need and cultural relevance was more important than what might offend God. Theaters became America's sanctuaries. Project, sound, speakers and microphones converted church worship spaces into theaters. Historic symbols of the Christian church were taken down or removed lest a seeker be offended. The Contemporary Church became incarnate and dwelt among us.

Contemporary Evangelicalism lacked any historic connection to the Bible or theology. Successful churches were now well-attended mega-churches. The mother of all mega-churches was Willow Creek in suburban Chicago founded by Bill Hybels. Church liturgy changed dramatically. Hymnals were out, screens offered words without notes. So the congregation needed to know the tune. They didn't. Essentially, the Sunday morning experience at Willow Creek and its clones seemed more like a well-marketed George Whitefield outdoor revival than an ordered liturgy of historic Christianity. That is, Sunday morning worship was replaced by evangelism. The Sunday morning event was evangelistic; a midweek meeting was for the insiders who professed a commitment to Jesus as Savior. Self-help Eucharist along with a biblical sermon characterized the weeknight meeting. The midweek meeting was aimed at discipleship for Christians. A wide assortment of self-help ministries comprised the church including 12-step recovery programs and outreach involving justice, mercy and compassion for others.

Willow Creek came nowhere near meeting Luther's criteria for a Christian church. It was ministry posing as a church. No sacraments ever appeared during the morning worship service.

Confession and absolution were absent. In effect, a service at Willow Creek and other contemporary churches omitted elements essential to the historic Christian church and added culturally-accommodated features. Scot McKnight believed that megachurches had contributed to Evangelicalism's demise. We agree. Contemporary Evangelicalism's accommodation of secular culture into its ranks dumbed down the solemnity, joy and wonder of authentic worship. Like its ancestor Pietism, the Contemporary Church gravitated toward self-centeredness.

Existing denominational churches desired to buy into this latest fad of Evangelicalism and re-structure their Sunday morning experience to attract church shoppers looking for a reprieve from dry religion. But that left a group of other people who equated worship with hymnals, notes, words, religious symbols, historic hymns of the faith and a sermon derived from a biblical text. Pastors and church leaders were in a bind. They realized that this new contemporary mode would attract one segment of the religious market (not only young people) and then there would be those who wished to worship as they had for decades. So worship within a denominational church which was not contemporary was tagged traditional. Church signs rapidly changed to reflect the advent of two market-based types of service. A church sign might read, "Traditional Worship: 9:30AM, Contemporary Worship: 11:00AM." Aside from one's taste in music, drama, preaching, presence of absence of certain types of liturgy or any other aspect of customer satisfaction, this bipolar brand of worship created two churches under one roof. People who used to see one another in church, now did not. Community now depended upon the brand of worship you liked. Of course, this internal splitting of the church began years before when a congregation outgrew its sanctuary capacity and additional services were added. For those who didn't want to worship on Sundays, a special Saturday night service was created. This only added to the greater impossibility for Saturday worshipers to ever see Sunday worshipers. Ironically, community was fractured by worship within the Christian church. Another evidence of Gnosticism within Evangelicalism. It wasn't difficult to see how this phenomenon was a far cry from the intimacy of Christian fellowship in the early church. There is no suggestion from the Apostle Paul that the church needed to be relevant to its surrounding Greek-Roman culture in order to attract God-fearers into its worship services. If anything, Paul constantly challenged the churches he planted to be counter-cultural and to maintain their uniquely Christian identity as the body of Christ.

Several years into Willow Creek's existence its leadership decided to survey the congregation for its feedback on the new approach to liturgy, discipleship and outreach. The data overwhelmingly came back negative. People complained that no authentic discipleship existed. The Sunday morning experience didn't feed the needs for existing Christians to grow. The leadership, to their credit, recanted the original strategy of aiming the Sunday morning event to non-believers, the so-called seekers, and inserted more biblical and theological elements into the liturgy. However, to this day there still remains no biblical model for a bifurcated approach to worship which conducts two types of services: one on Sunday morning and another during the week both of which appear as church.

Beyond the worship conflict within a fractured church, non-biblical leadership styles came into being modeled more on the American corporation than from the Apostle Paul's advice to his understudy Timothy. Leadership Teams replaced boards of elders, deacons, and trustees. Leadership Teams were designed by specific functions. Each member of the ruling body had a job to perform in the church: worship, education, buildings and grounds, etc. A member of the team could feel satisfied that she did her job without helping shepherd the flock just so she could give a successful report at the monthly team meeting. Formerly, lay spiritual care of the church was handled by more biblically entitled groups called a session, elders or deacons. Elders or deacons interviewed new members, prayed for the church, visited the sick, and contacted those who they hadn't seen in church for a while. Shepherding the church now fell squarely upon the shoulders of the pastors, already overwhelmed with the duties of leading the church. A gradual erosion of history and tradition occurred over time. The titles of a church's historic denominational roots now appeared as the fine print on a church sign, or dropped altogether. *Community* replaced *church* on the signs. For example, First Baptist Church would now be called First Community Church (Baptist). Church worship, structure and signage reflected an organic shift in both liturgy, leadership and identity.

Another patriarch of the Contemporary Church was Rick Warren, pastor of Saddleback Church and author of best-selling *The Purpose Driven Life*. Some have considered his book a Christian catechism. However, the generic nature of his non-theological, gospel-challenged thoughts in this book recommend it as no more than populist self-help religion seasoned with feel-good theology. Devoid of mentioning sin, the cross, repentance, obedience and other biblical terms from church history, Warren's book takes its place alongside the self-help religion begun with Norman Vincent Peale's power of positive thinking and Robert Schuller's crystallized thoughts on self-actualization where Christ is optional. The contemporary church movement created space for an accommodation of culture and politics into the church. A phenomenon without precedent in the New Testament. In opposition to a contemporary church, there came into being a new paradigm for Evangelicalism—the Emergent Church whose poster child was Brian McClaren.

The Emergent Church

In his *The New Covenant of Ministry of the Holy Spirit*, Theologian Larry D. Pettigrew offers a succinct overview of evangelicalism's history:

> With the advent of neo-evangelicalism in the 1950s began a new movement among evangelicals that bases itself on human experience, minimizes the importance of doctrine, and neglects outward church relations. Since the Reformation, evangelicalism has undergone a number of paradigm shifts from classic evangelicalism,

Contemporary and Emergent Evangelicalism

> Pietism, fundamentalism and more recently [a mixture of fundamentalism and new evangelicalism]. Within evangelicalism, the emerging church has arisen as an attempt to serve the postmodern culture . . . that holds no absolutes . . . promotes pluralism and divergence. One of many voices recommends returning the church to medieval practices...others suggest departing from . . . . the role of Scripture and soteriology. The emerging church surprisingly says complimentary things about theological liberalism.

Emergent thinking challenged typical views of the new birth experience. While hardened Fundamentalists held fast to a traditional view of spiritual experience as the authority for one's faith, others suggested that the main weakness lay with elevating human experience as the main issue leading to a depreciation of doctrine, especially a theology of the church. Of course, this has been our theme throughout the book. Early in the twenty-first century we begin to see the signs of a waning Evangelicalism. D.G. Hart has even gone to the extent of suggesting that "Evangelicalism has to be relinquished as a religious identity because it does not exist. In fact it has been the wax nose of twentieth-century American Protestantism. Behind this proboscis . . . is a face void of any discernible features."[1]

Pettigrew even said that the emergent conversation, like the broader evangelical movement as a whole, is not primarily based on theology. The barrenness of all symbols and ritual in the contemporary theater needed to be replaced with the smells and bells of the medieval church, even if its doctrine of salvation was bankrupt.

The Emergent Church movement came and went quickly. Today, no one is talking about it. Like Evangelicalism itself, "the Emergent Church struggled for a clear definition."[2] Its founding fathers weren't sure about the term at all and either abandoned it altogether or tried to maintain its original meaning. Its short-lived

---

1. Hart, *Deconstructing Evangelicalism*, 16–17.
2. Stetzer, *Christianity Today*, 5–9.

existence as a conversation lasted hardly more than a decade. It was the first of Evangelicalism's many variants and emanations which scholars actually declared had no theological basis. It was inclusive, tolerant and preached love without a cross with its out-of-touch concept of sacrifice. Recall Luther's definition of a theology of the cross—calling a thing what it is. Nothing ever got that specific within the amoebic-shaped Emergent Church. As a clear example of the wide-open spectrum of postmodernism, McLaren's non-theological conversation about the church may be summed up in three words: relevance, reconstruction and revision.

Pundits of this movement continued the chat about relevance within Evangelicalism. At all costs, things needed to not only engage, but also accommodate cultural values of the present time. The church needed to be relevant. Church attendees needed to feel comfortable inside worship spaces. At the same time, unlike the Contemporary Church, emergent church thinking would include a rare look back at ancient rituals in non-Protestant traditions. Eastern Orthodoxy was embraced by students brought up in Bible churches. Roman Catholicism's sacraments were no longer anathema. An Evangelical version of monastic spirituality surfaced with *lectio divina* and Taize services. Relevant emergent churches had their own spiritual directors. In effect, McLaren's church was merely a later application of church growth theory from the earlier days of Neo-Evangelicalism. At all costs the new target audience of GenXers (ages 18–35) needed to be retained by the church. The old labels of liberal, conservative, maybe even Evangelical were shown the door. Earlier we spoke of church signage as reflective of emanations within evangelicalism. Denominational labels like Methodist and Baptist gave way to *community, fellowship,* or *kingdom*. At least these terms were reminiscent of Christian concepts.

Now, however to be relevant new terms arrived on the scene with no theological root: *sextant, mountaintop,* or *wellwater*. These churches peddled their own brand.

Revisionists were intellectually honest about their actual dismissal of historic church dogma. Was there really a place called Hell where the unsaved spent eternal separation from God's presence?

If sacrifice no longer computed with the intended audience, was the cross necessary for salvation? Didn't the Incarnation allow for the good in all religions to be on equal footing with Christianity? The list could go on. The importance here is that for the first time within some variant of Evangelicalism, the very doctrines of the Bible which launched classic Evangelicalism were challenged as obsolete. Evangelicalism now required palliative hospice care. The only treatment left was to keep the patient comfortable.

In this chapter we've analyzed the Contemporary Church and its opposing Emergent Church. Each of these emanations of Evangelicalism represent the end of a long list of reactionary movements. Like previous movements, they are attempts to re-invent Christianity. Beginning with Fundamentalism's withdrawal from culture, Neo-Evangelicalism's engagement with culture, we've just discussed how the Contemporary and Emergent Churches effectively accommodated culture to the extent that one wasn't always sure where church began and culture ended within each syncretism. Eventually no exit from culture or politics existed and Evangelicalism completely lost any theological identity. When culture as its host fell ever-deeper into Gnosticism, its three-hundred year old parasite followed suit going from life support to palliative care. Smatterings of piety showed up here and there as morphine drips designed to keep the patient comfortable. In the following chapter, we'll see how absorption by a Gnostic culture led to the death of this well-meaning homeless three-hundred year-old movement.

Chapter 12

The Death of Evangelicalism

THIS CHAPTER IS THE CLIMAX of the book. We've been saying that Evangelicalism is at best vulnerable to Gnostic influence and at worst a particular type of Gnosticism. We'll get into this discussion now by reviewing Gnosticism, by taking another look at the biblical aspects of the gospel and the church, and by summarizing how Evangelicalism succumbed to Gnostic distortions of human beings, salvation and the church. We've described Gnosticism according to the following:

1. An evil god created evil matter including the human body which is evil.
2. We can know God only through special experiences and knowledge.
3. All reality is a dualism. Gnosticism always splits reality; it is never holistic.
4. Sin doesn't exist. Humanity's problem is ignorance.
5. Salvation is the energizing of the divine spark within us.
6. Gnosticism has no church.

Let's then review the major biblical aspects of the *gospel and the church* stated below:

1. The good God created the human body in his image; Incarnation: God became flesh
2. God is known by grace through the Holy Spirit who witnesses with our spirit.
3. The Father, Son and Holy Spirit are one; person is one body, mind, soul, and spirit.
4. Sin is humanity's problem.
5. Salvation is by grace through faith in victory over sin and death accomplished by the death and resurrection of Jesus Christ who is both Savior and Lord of the universe
6. The church is a community, the body of Christ, where the Holy Spirit is present among recovering sinners participating with God's mission in the world.

Finally, we summarize the Gnostic distortions within Evangelicalism:

1. It distorted God's creation of human beings in his image by reducing a person to a sinner-only.
2. It demeaned the human body and offered no category for its salvation favoring the redeeming of lost souls only.
3. It defined salvation as an experience outside the church.
4. It sinned against the body of Christ by leaving the church.

We begin with a re-statement of David Bebbington's definition of Evangelicalism as *conversionism, biblicism, crucicentrism,* and *activism*. We note how this definition has misrepresented a Scriptural view the gospel.

First, conversionism has been defined by the mistranslation born again, from John's Gospel. Second, biblicism, while correctly positioning the Scripture as authority, was often subordinated to experience within Evangelicalism. Concerns *about* the Bible often took precedence over *what* the Scriptures actually said. Third, crucicentrism, though rightly positioning the cross at the center as that place where Jesus Christ *took the place* of sinners, left out the vicarious work of Christ *for us on our behalf*. Finally, while appropriately conveying a need for outreach, activism is an inadequate representation of the church's participation with Christ's mission to the world. The Great Commission commanded the church to go, make disciples, baptize and teach. It is the only mandate given to the church. That said, when Jesus equated himself to the poor, homeless, hungry and imprisoned, he spoke of social justice as the gospel of the Kingdom of God. Jesus' view of salvation is inclusive—it redeems both human and spiritual need. Jesus offers the Gospel to the whole person.

In this chapter our focus will be on the four statements above indicative of how Gnosticism distorted the Bible, gospel and the church.

First, we begin with the concept of the human being as a person created in the image of God with worth, dignity and value. Evangelicalism betrays itself by its vocabulary as we've noted throughout. To listen carefully to how this movement has spoken of the person is to hear little about the dignity ascribed to all human beings. Human beings are the closest representation of God on earth. Imagine the Trinity talking among itself about the creation of humanity. "Let us make human beings in our image, in our likeness . . . to rule . . . to be fruitful and multiply . . . to fill the earth and subdue it."[1] By definition, human beings, without becoming God, represent him in relationship to the rest of Creation. God gave power to women and men to rule the earth in a relationship with him. Despite all distortions, God's intention for his created world remains the same today, even after the entrance of sin and evil causing the damage to persons, animals and plants. Evangelicalism's contribution to the Gnosticism in our culture today is that it rarely articulated the value of the whole person. Rather, it typically spoke of saving lost souls. Let's now consider how Gnosticism splits the human being into pieces—body and spirit.

Second, Evangelicalism not only failed to view a human being as created with dignity in the image of God, it also reduced the human being to spirit-only by demeaning the human body.

---

1. Genesis 1:26

This error has huge theological implications for the Incarnation where God decides to enter his own creation in the same way any human being did. The Word became flesh. Christmas doesn't exist without the Incarnation. Jesus of Nazareth was simultaneously a human being and the Second person of the Trinity, the Son of God. For now, we need to explore this sad scissoring of a human being into the piece parts of flesh and spirit. As earlier stated, this problem begins with an errant theological view of creation and extends to a misinformed theology of the body. Both aspects have Gnostic implications where matter is evil which means the human body is evil. Evangelicalism dealt with the issue of sin, as it should have. However, it did so at the expense of a biblical theology of the person as an integration of flesh, mind, soul, and spirit.

Jesus never rubbed a person's nose in his sin. He didn't need to make a person into a sinner first to then save them. He knew all about sin and sinners. He also realized that deep in one's heart, a person knows something's wrong, even if they express it in non-theological terms. When questioned with "Who sinned this man or his father?" Noting that this was the wrong question, Jesus deflected it into a conversation about the glory of God. When doubted as one who could forgive sin, Jesus equated healing the body with forgiving sin in one act of redemption resulting in a forgiven paralytic who got up and walked away. Throughout his ministry, Jesus always took the needs of the whole person seriously. A thirsty woman at a well needed healing in her marital relationships as well as in her spiritual way to worship. The Samaritan was good not because he was on his way to a Bible study, but because he tended to the human needs associated with being beaten up requiring immediate medical care and housing.

Twentieth century theology was characterized by a constant misunderstanding of the holistic gospel of Jesus Christ. Liberals tended the human needs and reduced the gospel to sociality. Fundamentalists-become-evangelicals reacted against liberals and preached a pseudo-gospel which saved bodiless souls. Neither proclaimed the good news of Jesus. Gnosticism was inherent in each distortion. For the liberals against whom Evangelicals reacted, the human being was a spiritless body. For Evangelicals, the human being was a bodiless spirit. Theologically, the issue has always been a distortion or absence of a biblical view of both Creation and the human being. Focusing on Evangelicalism, it would have been better to trade off endless inerrancy conversations about the length of a day for a more theological reading of Genesis to solve these first two issues which accommodated a Gnostic view of the human being. One's theology of creation and the body directly impacts how one speaks of salvation.

Third, Evangelicalism embarked upon a catch-phrase rendition of the gospel in its use of language foreign to the Word of God. This issue is most blatant in how Jesus was viewed as divided into two beings: Savior and then, Lord. Merely from a quantitative view, *Savior* needs only two-thirds of a column in the index of my Bible. *Lord* requires ten columns of verses. But this only gets the ball rolling. Just as born again is a mistranslation of John 3: 3, the catch-phrase for salvation, *accept Jesus as your Savior* is a misinterpretation of the gospel. To repeat, the Bible nowhere offers salvation by merely accepting Jesus as one's Savior. If Evangelicalism must die for any reason, it needs to be for this bumper-sticker reduction of the most important event in a person's life. Jesus never said a person must be born again. Peter didn't offer salvation by accepting Jesus into one's heart as a personal Savior. The Apostle Paul never discussed a theology of salvation using Evangelicalism's reductionist vocabulary. If Jesus isn't grasped as Lord, he will never become your Savior. Paul settles this in Romans 10: 9–10 where he speaks of salvation only when one confesses that Jesus is Lord along with a sincere belief in the resurrection. You don't accept Jesus; you confess him as Lord, the center of the Universe and focal point of your life. Yes, salvation is a gift to be received; but confession implies the action of following. Jesus becomes your Savior when you finally decide to agree with God that He is Lord and take up his cross to follow as a disciple. The gospel, the good news, began on earth with Jesus' first words, "Repent and believe the good news!" *Repent* means change your lifestyle. Jesus must be embraced, confessed and believed in as our *Lord* Jesus Christ.

The Death of Evangelicalism

Fourth, Evangelicalism demeaned the body of Christ by abandoning the church. *There is no salvation outside the church.* Stated differently, there is no salvation outside the body of Christ. This does not mean that only an organized tradition of Christianity can offer salvation. It doesn't mean that only Baptists can be saved. It doesn't mean that only the Catholic Church offers the true way to become a Christian. It certainly doesn't mean that only Evangelicals possess the esoteric knowledge of salvation. *There is no salvation outside the church* means that the process of being saved is not complete until and unless one is an active participant in a local congregation of fellow Christ-followers. Paul wrote letters to churches, not individuals.

In sum, Evangelicalism fell prey to Gnostic thought in its reduction of a person to sinner-only, its dualistic splitting of the person into a body versus a spirit, its splitting of Jesus into a Savior and Lord, and its abandonment the Word who became flesh when it left Christ's body, the church.

Throughout its life, *Evangelicalism was a para-church movement* of associations, societies, alliances, student movements, publishers, colleges and seminaries. Without the authority of a local congregation submitted to a biblical structure of apostles, bishops, elders, deacons, pastors, teachers and evangelists, it went its own way as a homeless assortment of religious persons. When so-called Evangelical churches got in trouble, they had no appeal to a hierarchy of spiritual counsel and were left to solve their own problems. Such churches ultimately imploded and died symptomatic of the movement itself. Lacking accountability, one-man Evangelical alliances and associations fell by the wayside without needed outside intervention from a structure of accountability.

Finally, Evangelicalism has always had its dark side, "its 'spiritual conceit,' ecclesiastical isolationism . . . and pessimism about both the world and the church . . . "[2] McGrath challenges the movement for generating its share of burned out pastors and walking wounded. He claims that Evangelicalism sustains doubt by its incessant need for reassurance. Evangelicalism has been

2. McGrath, *Evangelicalism and the Future of Christianity*, 147–65.

characterized by an inability to major in the majors, and not in the minors. Evangelicals have too often spent more time defending themselves to one another rather than to defend the faith to the world. Adhering to party lines results when core truths are compromised. Finally, Evangelicals have been as vulnerable to any magnetic orators who emerge over time as a personality cult. Media communication in all its forms has communicated a growing number of narcissists masquerading as proclaimers of the gospel. Self-help religion has replaced God's grace. History has produced a dangerous number of charismatic orators. To summarize, spiritual pride, doubt, in-grown critique and religious personality cult have been nails in Evangelicalism's coffin. Evangelicalism is beyond repair and needs to vanish.

The good news is Jesus Christ is alive as the only way to God. His body, the church, is the only true human community left on earth. We next consider how removing the cataract of Evangelicalism from Christianity creates a clearer vision of both the gospel and the church for the twenty-first century.

Chapter 13

The Twenty-First Century Church

THE CHRISTIAN CHURCH ENTERED THE TWENTY-FIRST CENTURY in dysfunction. In part, its need for recovery stems from Evangelicalism's three-hundred-year distortion of the gospel and neglect of the church. We've blamed Gnosticism. The Christian church needs to heal from the infection of a Gnostic-influenced Evangelicalism. As in any recovery, the first step is admission that one is powerless to change on its own and requires a higher power. That higher power is the Holy Spirit capable of reforming and reviving the church. Its reformation will be a return to the Word. Its revival will be a fresh encounter with the Holy Spirit. The church must admit that it is broken and needs a contrite heart. The church needs to admit that is powerless to overcome Evangelicalism requiring an outside intervention. We now attempt to identity those elements of the church which require healing and recovery such that it may not only survive, but flourish beyond our century. In sum, a recovery of the twenty-first century church depends upon both Word and Spirit.

Both Word and Spirit originate outside the church. The church needs to be born from above by the Holy Spirit as Jesus told Nicodemus. The church needs to be more overtly counter-cultural as American society continues to endure fragmentation and deterioration rooted in narcissistic Gnosticism. The church needs to embrace a theological grasp of itself and the core doctrines which define its uniqueness as the *already, but not yet* kingdom of God. At the beginning of his ministry, Jesus said the kingdom of God is at hand. He also stated that the kingdom of God is within you. The church needs to see itself as ushering in the Kingdom of God.

Gnostic-Evangelicalism must be named. It must be called what it is—the wolf in sheep's clothing. It must be called out. Its doctrine of creation, humanity and the body as evil must be surgically removed from the church. The teaching of creation, humanity and the body as God's goodness must be proclaimed and lived out. The church must teach that all human beings are created in the image of God with dignity, worth and value reflecting the image of a Triune God. Only then must it inform persons how they've been tainted by sin, the inherited demon who continues to destroy lives.

The salvation of human beings begins with an understanding that a person is a holistically integrated organism designed to love God in body, mind, soul, and spirit. The recovering church must admit that it is broken in body, mind, soul, and spirit. A result of such salvation must show up in the concrete love of one's neighbor in physical, mental and spiritual ways. It must love itself as Christ loves it challenging the self-centered narcissistic self-love running rampant today. Loving one's neighbor equals loving Jesus who is embodied in the hungry, thirsty, sick, lonely, homeless and imprisoned. Jesus doesn't merely care for human beings at the periphery of society, he *is* that person as recovering tax collector Matthew tells us. That church needs to grasp the gospel as a seamless remedy both for lost souls and fractured bodies represented by human beings. Just as Jesus is one person in two natures, a human being is one person spiritually severed from a relationship with God, mentally detached from thinking God's thoughts and behaviorally impaired. Only a holistic gospel has the power to dismantle a dualistic Gnosticism's destruction of a person and the church.

Catholic theologian George Weigel accurately views Evangelicalism as an impoverishment of Christian experience. He calls for a renewed church which is incarnate—God's flesh on earth. All that God was in coming to earth as a human being models what the church can be as the new humanity spoken of by the Apostle Paul. Weigel challenges the church to not merely *have* a mission, but to *be* a mission. He calls for a church to be more herself and for Christians to be more the church in community, not as inward-focused individuals floating around in their little pious boats.

Brian McCracken rightly observes that the church has "historically thrived when she is tested rather than comfortable." He challenges Christians to read their Bibles. His rejection of Gnosticism encourages the church to become a people re-sensitized to the fleshly incarnation of the body of Christ in the world. He translates *This is my body* into a participation in the body and blood of Christ on earth. Oswald Chambers would state it this way: the church needs to become broken bread and poured out wine for others. Paul Fiddes would view Christians as living sacraments seasoning the earth as a scattered community having been nourished at the Table as a gathered congregation.

Christianity Today's Mark Galli calls for a more Catholic and Orthodox Protestant church. Uncharacteristically traditional for an Evangelical, he urges an evangelistic piety rooted in historic Augustinian spirituality. The mere mention of a tradition prior to the eighteenth century Great Awakenings is a step in the right direction. A healthy move in the church today is its freedom to explore Catholic spirituality.

Frank Viola's *Reimagining the Church* provactively suggests that fellowship is *not* one of the reasons for a church meeting. Mutual edification and exhortation are. He cites 1 Corinthians 14: 26, "When you come together, each of you has a psalm, doctrine, tongue, revelation and interpretation. Let all things be done to edify." He says that preaching is not the central event of Christian liturgy. He wants more informal communal conversation around the Word and open communication to encourage one another. Viola calls for a practical priesthood of all believers applied to meetings of the church-community. His incarnational church flows from what should be the central event of church meetings—Eucharist. He advocates meeting in homes, rather than in sanctuaries.

Evangelicalism Is Dead

In one way or another, the previous suggestions are offered as steps toward recovery from Gnosticism's grip on the church. Its divine spark is replaced by the indwelling of Holy Spirit of God, the third member of the Trinity. It's denial of the body is replaced by the biblical view of the human body as a creation in God's likeness. The church is seen as the body of Christ; as an incarnation of God on earth in a visible and concrete way. Gnosticism's dualisms are replaced by a holistic integration of the human being as body, mind, soul, and spirit. The Christian can then obey Jesus' mandate to love God with all its strength, mind, soul, and spirit. The grace of God in Christ at the cross of Jesus replaces esoteric knowledge as the way of salvation.

We conclude this chapter with an appeal to the robust statements about the church from Scripture, historic tradition, and reason as the basis for a spiritually healthy church. That is, we view a reformed and revived theology of the church as an alternative to Bebbington's definition of Evangelicalism.

The first documented theological description of the church community occurs in Acts 2: 42–47. Luke tells us that after baptism the first Christians gathered together for worship, instruction and fellowship. They gathered together. No one thought of exercising a new-found faith alone. They celebrated the Lord's Supper as Jesus had commanded the day before he died—in community. They prayed with and for one another gathered as one new humanity of the cross. They made sure everyone's human needs were met. Having your own material needs met wasn't enough. The results were phenomenal—reverence, awe, miracles and supernatural signs of God's presence among them. Their behaviors were unashamedly counter-cultural. People flocked to their community. The church grew by seeing people transfer from the kingdom of evil to the kingdom of the Spirit; not be merely transferring memberships from one church to another. They really believed Jesus' words about the church: Christ is the rock, the cornerstone, of a community committed to forgiveness in all relationships. A regular practice of the Lord's Supper assured taking their temperature as a community. Who needed to confess? Who required forgiveness?

The Twenty-First Century Church

Was the community at peace? If so, only then could the community could take the bread and wine. May the twenty-first century church rediscover these essentials of a healthy community of recovering sinners admitting brokenness as the precondition for possessing a contrite heart.

Historically, the next documented theology of the church comes from the Apostle Paul's letters to churches. His signature theology of church community is summed in one word: the unified body of those in Christ. From his letter to Roman Christians regarding spiritual gifts, he says "so in Christ we who are many form one body." In his Corinthian correspondence offering both liturgical and practical advice, he re-states his concept of the church stating this: "Now the body is not made up of one part but of many . . . there should be no division in the body . . . its parts should have equal concern for each other. If one part suffers, every part suffers with it; if one part is honored, every part rejoices with it." In Galatians, Paul restates how the body cares for itself. "Carry each other's burdens and in this way you will fulfil the law of Christ." One of his most profound statements of the church occurs in his letter to the Ephesian church. Constructing an ecclesiology from the cross, he writes, "through his blood . . . [Christ] . . . has made the two [Jew and Gentile] one by abolishing in his flesh the law with its commandments and regulations . . . to create in himself one new humanity out of the two." Here we have the theological basis for ethnic diversity in the church. May the twenty-first century church strive together to tear down that dividing wall between all races and cultures. The rationale for ethnic diversity within the church originates from Scripture, not from cultural or political correctness.

Next, we note how the Apostle Paul builds his theology of the church from the cross. Bonhoeffer's vicarious Christ comes from this statement: "Now I rejoice in what was suffered for you, and I fill up in my flesh what is still lacking in regard to Christ's afflictions, for the sake of his body, the church."[1] The church takes up a ministry of reconciliation of the world. A Christian is a totally

---

1. Colossians 1:24

different person involved in God's mission on earth. Here we have Bonhoeffer's *Christ existing as the church* for others. May a reformed and revived twenty-first century church be Christ for the church and the world.

We mention again Martin Luther's seven-point marks of the church: Scripture, baptism, Eucharist, the keys of confession-forgiveness, ordination of pastors and church leaders, praise and thanksgiving in worship and in prayer and the cross. Here we have a definition of the church from Scripture worth fighting for. May the reformed twenty-first century church exhibit these behaviors which answer Luther's paraphrased question—"Where can I find the church?"

John Calvin was a systematic theologian. From his *Institutes*, he says that the visible church is the womb which gives us birth. Note that rebirth originates from the church, not from an individual experience or decision. It nourishes us and keeps us under her charge and government, until, divest of mortal flesh, we become like the angels. Beyond the pale of the church, no forgiveness of sins, no salvation can be hoped for. Once again, the process of salvation continues in the church. No valid profession of individual Christian faith is detached from membership in a church community. The most obvious sign of a genuine commitment to Jesus Christ as Lord is participation in the body and blood of Christ. Continuing in his *Institutes*, Calvin continues, "God regards as deserters all who alienate themselves from the true ministry of His word and sacraments. To violate the Church impairs the authority of God."[2] When Evangelicals left the church, they detached themselves from God's word. They deserted God. When they exited the church, they replaced God's authority. They became those who said, "Lord, Lord" to whom God says "I never knew you." May twenty-first century Christians remain in the church despite its warts and wounds. May we reattached ourselves to God's Word rather than deserting God and his authority in our lives.

The Church is the pillar and ground of truth. In our postmodern, post-Christian culture, appeal to truth has vanished.

---

2. Calvin, *Institutes*, 670–89.

Today, merely having a nice-sounding narrative is all one needs to validate an idea. Jesus Christ is the way, truth and the life. He is the only way to the Father. His is the only name by which we can be saved. May the twenty-first century church be a recovering church reformed by the Word of God and revived by the Holy Spirit.

Conclusion

WE'VE ASSERTED THAT EVANGELICALISM, a three-hundred year-old Protestant movement, is dead. Rooted in the Reformation, it marginalized the Bible. Singing about the cross, it later found sacrifice irrelevant to the times. Proclaiming the gospel, it removed sin and repentance from its vocabulary. Speaking about a Great Commission, it generated converts without making disciples.

David Bebbington defined the movement with these four terms: *biblicism, crucicentrism, conversionism* and *activism*. Each term locates Evangelicalism within a Christian context but only partially represents a theological treatment of the gospel. Bebbington accurately defines the movement by leaving out any mention of the church. Because Evangelicalism left the church and became parasitic in its relationship to it as its host. Without the church, Evangelicalism finds itself in the dubious position to claim being Christian while simultaneously omitting God's chosen vehicle for ushering in the kingdom of God.

Taking a fresh theological approach to the gospel and the church, we next analyzed an arch enemy of Christianity, Gnosticism. We saw how the Apostle John warned the church about how Gnosticism masquerades as Christianity by sounding spiritual. We noted that Evangelicalism is vulnerable to this heresy which presents salvation as a spiritually-enhanced inner divine spark. Sadly, we pointed out that Evangelicalism itself became a conveyor of Gnostic thought.

In our brief overview of Evangelicalism's history we consistently noted an addiction to personal experience termed by *born again*—a mistranslation of Scripture. We said that experience in and of itself is unverifiable. Personal experience cannot be an intellectually-compelling reason to consider God's gracious offer of salvation. We noted that the results of any Great Awakening, Graham crusade or any other mass evangelism yielded little impact on the church. Evangelicalism's contra-church attitude originated with the mass revivalism associated with George Whitfield, Charles Finney and D.L. Moody. It continues to this day, as many Evangelicals bow to a consumer-centric subculture as seekers looking for customer satisfaction as they shop for church. Glorifying one's religious appetites may be satiated by a certain brand of spiritual experience, but consumerism falls short of authentic worship of God.

Evangelicalism got caught up in debates over issues peripheral to a sincere study *of* God's Word, choosing rather to argue *about* the Bible. Mass revivals outside the church reduced the gospel to saving bodiless souls. This mongrel gospel triggered a reaction by theological liberalism to reduce the gospel to soul-less bodies. Jesus viewed people as internally conflicted between body and spirit. Jesus viewed the human being created in God's image as an integration of body, mind, soul, and spirit. He gave his life for the destruction of sin upon God's image and its distortion of body, mind, soul, and spirit. The cross creates hope for sinners to recover from sin's destruction by becoming reshaped into the image of Christ. Christ's image restores us to the image of God intended by creation.

It offers the power to live without sinning. It offers the grace of forgiveness when we do sin.

The twentieth century began with the militant reduction of the gospel combatting modernism and liberalism in a five-point anti-intellectual approach to Christianity called Fundamentalism. This movement set back any good that classic Evangelicalism may have achieved as a dominant American religious phenomenon in the late seventeenth and early eighteenth centuries. One reduction of the faith triggered another called Neo-Evangelicalism. Billy Graham and others made an attempt to engage culture as atonement

Conclusion

for Fundamentalism's separatism. However well-intentioned at restoring intellectualism to this homeless movement, Neo-evangelicalism's try at engaging culture did not end well. Evangelicalism's addiction to relevance went way beyond cultural engagement. Early in the twenty-first century, relevance led to accommodation resulting in absorption by culture. The movement hitched its wagon to culture in its rejection of the church. Having been originally attached to the church as a parasite, it found a new host in American culture. Only that culture was thoroughly Gnostic and narcissistic. Evangelicalism evidenced this Gnosticism by its personality cult of pastors and leaders, ingrown piety and a declining energy to fulfill the Great Commission. Ultimately, Evangelicalism's activism, not to be confused with *Missio Dei*, found itself attached to yet another host, American politics. This was a return to Fundamentalism represented by Falwell's Moral Majority, where ethics and morality were substituted for the gospel. At this writing, the movement is more identified with politics than religion. Evangelical leaders have precariously aligned themselves with the Oval office. In *Still Evangelical?* Mark Labberton says that for many people *evangelical* no longer refers to a set of theological commitments but to a "theo-political brand." Labberton's robust phrase is a book in itself.

A growing number of former Evangelicals call themselves post-Christian. A few scholars now question whether Evangelicalism ever existed. Those who acknowledge its existence now call for its deconstruction. As a parasite, it destroyed the church. As a cataract, it blurred the gospel. It imploded and turned in on itself. It died. May the death of Evangelicalism create space to resurrect both the pure gospel and a vital church in United States. Resonating with Dietrich Bonhoeffer, may the living Christ exist as the church; and may that renewed church exist for others.[1]

---

1. Bonhoeffer, *Letters and Papers from Prison*, 503.

Bibliography

Ahlstrom, Sydney E., *The Religious History of the American People*, London: Yale Press, 1972.
Anderson, Matthew Lee, "(How) Are Evangelicals Gnostic?" *Mere Orthodoxy* 16–19 (June 2010).
Anyabwile, Thabiti, "Evangelical Gnosticism," feeds.feedburner.com/Pure ChurchBlog, (2018).
Baker, Mark D., and Joel B. Green, eds., *Recovering the Scandal of the Cross: Atonement in New Testament and Contemporary Contexts*, Second Edition, Downers Grove: Intervarsity, 2011.
Baker, William R., ed., *Evangelicalism & The Stone-Campbell Movement*, Downers Grove: Intervarsity, 2002.
Balmer, Randall, *Evangelicalism in America*, Waco: Baylor University Press, 2016.
Barth, Karl, "The Being of Community." In *Volume IV. The Doctrine of Reconciliation, Church Dogmatics* 341–65. Edinburgh: T&T Clark, 1956.
Bebbington, David W., *Evangelicalism in Modern Britain: A History from the 1730s to the 1980s*, London: Unwin Hyman, 1989.
Bloom, Harold, *The American Religion: The Emergence of the Post-Christian Nation*, New York: Touchstone, 1992.
Boersma, Hans, *Scripture as Real Presence*, Grand Rapids: Baker, 2017.
Bonhoeffer, Dietrich, *Discipleship*, G.B. Kelly and John Godsey, eds., DBWE, Volume 4, Minneapolis: 2000.
———. *Letters and Papers from Prison*, John W. De Gruchy, ed., DBWE, Volume 8, Minneapolis: 2010.
———. *Life Together-Prayerbook of the Bible*, G.B. Kelly, ed., DBWE, Volume 5, Minneapolis: 1996.
———. *Sanctorum Communio*, Clifford Green, ed., DBWE, Volume 1, Minneapolis: 1998.
Burfeind, Peter M., *Gnostic America*, Toledo, Ohio: Pax Domini, 2014.
Calvin, John, "Book Fourth: Of the Holy Catholic Church." In *Institutes of the Christian Religion* 734–41 Peabody, Massachusetts: Hendrickson, 2012.

Bibliography

Chalke, Steven, "Evangelicalism and the Future," https://www.christianitytoday.com/article/evangelicalism-and-the-future/38474.htm (2014).

Clemenger, Bruce, "Our Evangelical Neighbors," www.cccb.ca/site/images/stories/pdf/CCCB_Our_Neighbors_e-web.pdf (2016).

Davidson, Bruce W., "The Death of Evangelicalism," *American Thinker* (2016).

Douglas, Mary and Steven M. Tipton, eds., *Religion and America*, Boston: Beacon, 1983.

Favale, Abigail Rine, "Evangelical Gnosticism," The Aquila Report, http://the aqiulareport.com/evangelical-gnosticism/2018.

Fiddes, Paul, *Participating in God: A Pastoral Doctrine of the Trinity*, Louisville, Kentucky: Westminster John Knox, 2000.

Fitzgerald, Frances, *The Evangelicals: The Struggle to Shape America*, New York, Simon & Schuster, 2017.

Galli, Mark, "Revival at Cane Ridge," https://christianhistoryinstitute.org/magazine/article/revival-at-cane-ridge/2019.

Gathercole, Simon J., *The Pre-existent Son*, Grand Rapids: Eerdmans, 2006.

Guinness, Oz, "Is Evangelicalism Outdated," https://virtualonline.org/evangelicalism-outdated/2018.

Hart, D. G., *Deconstructing Evangelicalism*, Grand Rapids: Baker Academic, 2004.

Hatch, Nathan O., *The Democratization of American Christianity*, New Haven: Yale University Press, 1989.

Henry, Carl F. H., *Architect of Evangelicalism*, Bellingham, WA: Lexham, 2019.

———. *The Uneasy Conscience of Modern Fundamentalism*, Grand Rapids: Eerdmans, 1947.

Howard, Carol Merritt, "Why Evangelicalism is Failing a Generation," https://huffpost.com/entry/why-evangelicalism-is-failing-a-new-generation/503971 (2010).

Howard, Thomas, *Evangelical Is Not Enough*, San Francisco: Ignatius, 1984.

Hybels, Lynn and Bill, *Rediscovering the Church: The Story and Vision of Willow Creek Community Church*, Grand Rapids: Zondervan, 1995.

Jenkins, Philip, *The Next Christendom*, Third Edition, Oxford: Oxford University Press, 2011.

John Paul II, Pope, *Man and Woman He Created Them: A Theology of the Body*, Boston: Pauline Books, 2006.

Jonas, Hans, *The Gnostic Religion*, Second Edition, Boston: Beacon, 1963.

Kantzer, Kenneth S. and Carl F. Henry, eds., *Evangelical Affirmations*, Grand Rapids: Zondervan, 1990.

Kidd, Thomas, *Who is an Evangelical? A History of a Movement in Crisis*, New Haven: Yale University Press, 2019.

Labberton, Mark, ed., *Still Evangelical? Insiders Reconsider Political, Social, and Theological Meaning*, Downers Grove: Intervarsity, 2018.

Lee, Philip J., *Against the Protestant Gnostics*, Oxford: Oxford University Press, 1987.

BIBLIOGRAPHY

Luther, Martin, *The Bondage of the Will*, Translated by J. I. Packer & O. R. Johnston, Grand Rapids: Fleming Revell, 1957.
———. *Martin Luther's Basic Theological Writings*, ed., Timothy F. Lull, Minneapolis: Fortress, 1989.
Machen, J. Gresham, *Christianity and Liberalism*, Grand Rapids: Eerdmans, 2009.
Marsden, George, *Evangelicalism and Modern America*, Grand Rapids: Eerdmans, 1984.
———. *Fundamentalism and American Culture*, Second Edition, Oxford: Oxford University Press, 2006.
———. *Understanding Fundamentalism and Evangelicalism*, Grand Rapids: Eerdmans, 1991.
Marty, Martin E., "The Years of the Evangelicals." *Christian Century*, 5 (1989) 22 – 24.
McGrath, Alister, *Christianity's Dangerous Idea*, New York: HarperCollins, 2007.
———. *Evangelicalism and the Future of Christianity*, London: Hodder & Stoughton, 1993.
Neuhaus, Richard John, ed., *The Second One Thousand Years*, Grand Rapids: Eerdmans, 2001.
Noll, Mark A., *American Evangelical Christianity: An Introduction*, Malden: Blackwell, 1991.
———. *America's God: From Jonathan Edwards to Abraham Lincoln*, Oxford: Oxford University Press, 2002.
———. *The Rise of Evangelicalism: The Age of Edwards, Whitefield and the Wesleys*, Downers Grove: Intervarsity, 2003.
———. *The Scandal of the Evangelical Mind*, Grand Rapids: Eerdmans, 1994.
Packer, J. I., ed., *Evangelicals Today*, London: Lutterworth, 1973.
Pettigrew, Larry, *The New Covenant Ministry of the Holy Spirit*, Lanham, MD: University Press of America, 1993.
Roberts, Alastair J., "What Is Evangelicalism?" https://alastairadversaria.com/2012/10/26/what-is-evangelicalism-part-1/.
Rudolph, Kurt, *Gnosis: The Nature and History of Gnosticism*, San Francisco: HarperCollins, 1987.
Ryrie, Alec, *Protestantism: The Radical Who Made the Modern World*, London: HarperCollins, 2017.
Schaeffer, Francis A., *The Great Evangelical Disaster*, Westchester, Illinois: Crossway, 1984.
Smedes, Lewis B. "Evangelicalism – A Fantasy," *Reformed Journal* (1980) 16–19.
Smith, Christian, *The Bible Made Impossible*, Grand Rapids: Bravos, 2012.
Stackhouse, Jr., John G., *Evangelical Landscapes: Facing Critical Issues of the Day*, Grand Rapids: Baker, 2002.
Stetzer, Ed, "The Emergent/Emerging Church: A Missiological Perspective." *Christianity Today* (2008) 34–38.
Taylor, Charles, *The Secular Age*, Cambridge: Harvard University Press, 2007.

BIBLIOGRAPHY

Viola, Frank, *Reimagining the Church: Pursuing the Dream of Organic Christianity*, Colorado Springs: David C. Cook, 2008.

Warfield, Benjamin, "In Behalf of Evangelical Religion." *Presbyterian* (1920) 3-7.

Warren, Tish Harrison, *Liturgy of the Ordinary*, Downers Grove: Intervarsity, 2016.

Webber, Robert E., *The Younger Evangelicals*, Grand Rapids: Baker, 2002.

Weber, Max., "The Sociology of Charismatic Authority," In *From Max Weber: Essays in Sociology*, 23-34. London: Oxford University Press, 1946.

Weigel, George, *Evangelical Catholicism: Deep Reform in the 21st-Century Church*, New York: Basic Books, 2013.

Wells, David F., *No Place for Truth, Or What Ever Happened to Evangelical Theology?*, Grand Rapids: Eerdmans, 1993.

Worthen, Molly, *Apostles of Reason: The Crisis of Authority in American Evangelicalism*, Oxford: Oxford University Press, 2014.

Zachman, Randall C., *The Assurance of Faith: Conscience in the Theology of Martin Luther and John Calvin*, Minneapolis: Fortress, 1993.

www.ingramcontent.com/pod-product-compliance
Lightning Source LLC
Chambersburg PA
CBHW070920160426
43193CB00011B/1533